WRITE-IN:

DIARY OF A CONGRESSIONAL CANDIDATE
IN FLORIDA'S FOURTH CONGRESSIONAL DISTRICT

WRITE-IN:

Diary of a Congressional Candidate
in Florida's Fourth Congressional District

Richard Grayson

Published in the United States by Dumbo Books,
Brooklyn, New York.

E-mail: dumbobooks@yahoo.com,
Richard.Grayson@yahoo.com

ISBN 978-0-6151-4111-4

First Edition

10 9 8 7 6 5 4 3 2 1

Acknowledgements

This diary of my 2004 campaign for Congress first appeared on the McSweeney's Internet Tendency website. I will forever be indebted to McSweeney's and especially to the editor of the website, John Warner, an estimable author in his own right (and not to be confused the Republican U.S. Senator from Virginia who married Elizabeth Taylor and dated Barbara Walters). John helped me focus the entries that make up this journal, provided crackerjack editorial advice, and allowed me to have a wider forum than I could have hoped for. Thank you, John.

I would also like to thank, for their encouragement, support and inspiration Professor Patrick M. Ellingham of Broward Community College; Dean Joseph Harbaugh of Nova Southeastern University Shepard Broad Law Center; Dean Kenneth Starr of Pepperdine University School of Law; Clarence Major; Susan Fromberg Schaeffer; Chris Carrabba; Earl Graves; Richard Peabody; Sharon Booth; Satnam Kaur Khalsa; Jerry Weinberger; Linda Konner; Kenneth Falk; Nina Mule; Randy Tunkel; Tom Whalen; Brian Pera; Linda Sawyer; Paul Schickler; Judd Lear Silverman; Mark Padin; Paul Fericano; Jonathan Baumbach; Stephen Elliott; former Florida House Speaker Jon Mills; former Representatives Steve Solarz and Elizabeth Holtzman; former Attorney General Ramsey Clark; Brooklyn Borough President Marty Markowitz; my friends at Readerville; my parents; and my brothers, Marc and Jonathan.

To the memory of
New York City Council President Paul O'Dwyer
– who taught me that politics could be fun and who
let me take Dorothy Parker's ashes out of his filing
cabinet

Prologue: Dumping the Hump in Chicago

As a senior at Brooklyn's Midwood High School in the spring of 1968, I divided my acquaintances as either Gene McCarthy people or Bobby Kennedy people although it was debatable which category I myself fit into. I was registered for Mr. Ilivicky's Social Studies class called Problems in American Democracy, and as part of the course, all the students had to work a couple of hours a week in the Manhattan office of Senator Kennedy.

But like a lot of kids, I came, as Time Magazine would have it, "clean for Gene" when Senator McCarthy announced he would run against President Johnson. Actually, my hair wasn't all that long, and I couldn't grow sideburns or a beard. I barely had any hair on my body. So I didn't have to become "clean." Nobody else besides McCarthy was running as a peace candidate for President.

Two years before, at 15, I worked for one of the first peace candidates to run for Congress, Mel Dubin, who was challenging longtime Brooklyn Representative Abe Multer in the Democratic primary. (There were no Republicans in Brooklyn).

Back in 1966, we had a whole antiwar slate of candidates for all the offices, including one guy who our campaign manager, Steve Solarz – who'd later hold the Congressional seat himself till he was

kicked out in the House banking scandal –
mistakenly recruited to run for the state senate
because the guy shared the same name as the man
he was told to recruit, a community leader and
chairman of a local B'nai B'rith chapter.

This character always showed up in tattered
jeans and a t-shirt with holes under the arms, but by
the time we realized we had promised the ballot
spot to the wrong person, this guy was our
candidate because Steve said it was too late to kick
him off the ticket because in politics, your word is
your bond.

Mel Dubin lost by a handful of votes, and in
1968 I was as determined as a 104-pound high
school student – short, skinny, bookish and
bespectacled, I kept hoping to be bitten by a
radioactive spider – could be to elect an antiwar
President. So when the McCarthy for President
headquarters opened on Flatbush Avenue, I signed
up.

Most of the other campaign workers were
college students or middle-aged Jewish women or
elderly ex-radicals from the 1930s. I was sort of
their mascot. I did everything from cranking the
mimeograph machine to make copies of our
newsletter ("You'll actually get biceps from that,"
one college girl told me) to cleaning the grimy toilet
and sink in the back of the store we were renting
month by month.

I also liked working in Senator Kennedy's office,

reading letters from people who wanted his help with an immigration problem or whatever and sending out thank you notes signed "Robert F. Kennedy" that were actually signed by a machine called the Autopen (which had three different signatures, so they weren't all exactly the same).

But when McCarthy did so well in the New Hampshire primary, and Bobby announced for President a few days later, I couldn't desert my first choice. Like Steve Solarz told me, in politics your word is your bond.

Still, the next few months after Johnson withdrew as a candidate for re-election were kind of hard because all the antiwar people in Brooklyn split between McCarthy and Kennedy. Kennedy won most of the primaries – people flocked to him, even if they were pro-war – but in Oregon, McCarthy scored an upset win. It was the first time a Kennedy had ever lost an election.

My seventeenth birthday was a week later, the day of the California primary. I stayed up long enough to find out that Bobby Kennedy had won, but I had to get up early so I didn't hear his speech – "Now it's on to Chicago and let's win there" – and didn't learn about his assassination till the next morning. I saw it on TV and began screaming, waking up everyone in the house. I couldn't stop crying. My dad said, "This lousy country, we should leave." It was exactly two months after Martin Luther King Jr. had been killed.

But of course we didn't leave. Three weeks later was the final primary, in New York, and many of our McCarthy delegates won. So did some Kennedy delegates. But by late July, it was clear that the nomination was going to Vice President Hubert Humphrey, who supported the war in Vietnam.

I so wanted to go to the convention in Chicago. There were going to be the biggest protest demonstrations ever at a political party meeting, and antiwar people from all over the country were converging in Mayor Daley's city the last week in August.

Most of the college kids and older people from the McCarthy HQ on Flatbush Avenue were going, and this older couple, the Hosenbooms, said they would watch out for me.

So I persuaded my parents to let me go. I made a sign for myself to carry. It said DUMP THE HUMP. Deep down, I was sure we could convince the party not to nominate a hawk like Humphrey because most Democrats were against the war.

My mom said I came back from Chicago a different kid.

It was really my first time away from my parents, and I saw stuff that was unimaginable.

I still pride myself on my terrific memory. You can quiz me on all sorts of things, from who was Brooklyn district attorney in 1971 (Aaron Koota) to what was the name of the drink that the teenaged George in "Who's Afraid of Virginia Woolf?" asked for in the bar (bergin), and I'll know it. But Chicago the last week of August 1968 is all a blur.

I can remember thousands of us gathered on Sunday in Lincoln Park in the city where Mayor Daley had ordered cops to "shoot to kill" during the April riots following Dr. King's assassination. Now he'd called in the National Guard to back up his police force, and the soldiers and cops suddenly told us to evacuate the park.

With tear gas and nightsticks and bayonets, they drove us out, chasing us for miles. Some of us threw rocks and bottles, breaking store windows on the way. The last I saw of Mrs. Hosenboom, her forehead was gushing blood.

Ending up in Grant Park across the street from the Conrad Hilton, where they had the only live TV cameras, we started chanting, "The whole world is watching."

What we didn't know was that Sunday night was that it was about to get a lot worse – and that the whole world, or most of it, would think we were about to get what we deserved.

I didn't start Brooklyn College that September like I was supposed to. I pretty much wanted to stay in my room. The truth was, I was afraid to go out. Afraid the world was too much like what I'd seen on the streets of Chicago. Afraid that a cop would beat me senseless the way they had Mrs. Hosenboom and so many others. Afraid that I'd have to run like hell and hide in someone's hotel room listening to the sounds of a riot, smelling the tear gas, watching people with bloody heads and clothes, people who'd just come there like I had, out of a belief that they could change things.

I mostly stayed in my room all fall and winter and early spring. I stirred out in May 1969, after these antidepressants and tranquilizers I'd been prescribed by my psychiatrist a couple of months before started to work. Mayor Lindsay was running for re-election, and they'd opened a campaign headquarters a few blocks from the old McCarthy storefront on Flatbush Avenue.

Lindsay was a liberal Republican when there was such a thing. He was much more liberal than any of the Democratic candidates for mayor with the exception of the writer Norman Mailer, who had no chance. Lindsay's natural constituency was liberal Democrats like my parents; he was especially loved in the black and Puerto Rican communities. None of these people, however, could vote in the June Republican primary.

Working in that storefront, I learned that there *were* Republicans in Brooklyn. Unfortunately, most of them hated John Lindsay. The morning after he lost the primary, I came to our headquarters feeling dejected.

When I saw that someone had spray-painted "Nigger Lover" all over our front door, I went to the store's bathroom in the back and cried, then brought out some Ajax and a wet rag and tried to wash the words away.

The next week I started going into Manhattan for the first time in a year. I hung out in Washington Square and even learned about what would become known as the Stonewall riot as it was happening from some lesbians who'd run over to the fountain where a lot of us young people were sitting.

By then my hair was down to my shoulders and I had long sideburns. I'd put on weight – from the antidepressants, I think. That July in Greenwich Village I was offered marijuana for the first time. I was ready for Woodstock in August and college in September. That fall I helped Mayor Lindsay win reelection as the candidate of the Liberal Party.

A few years later, I was cleaning out my closet and under a pile of old record albums and comic books and political posters, I found my DUMP THE HUMP sign.

In the melee – later termed a "police riot" by the Walker Commission – I'd somehow managed to hold onto the poster and bring it home from Chicago.

I didn't remember how I did it. I couldn't even remember anything about the bus ride from the Loop to downtown Brooklyn.

In the fall of 1995, while working as a staff attorney in social policy at a University of Florida think tank called the Center for Governmental Responsibility, I also had a part-time job teaching a college course called that met on Saturday mornings.

The course was called The Individual and Society.

One morning I showed the class Haskell Wexler's 1969 film *Medium Cool.* A fictional story about a reporter and an Appalachian woman and her young son during the Chicago convention, the movie also contains real scenes of the demonstrations.

At one point in *Medium Cool*, a canister of tear gas explodes, and if you listen carefully, you can hear someone in the background shout, "Look out, Haskell, it's real!"

My students could not believe such a thing could ever have happened in their country.

I told them how I knew it had.

I didn't go to Chicago again till 1997, when I had a residency at the Ragdale artists' colony in suburban Lake Forest. I really liked the city. I stopped associating it with what happened in 1968.

The last time I was in Chicago, was in June 2001, when I gave a reading at Quimby's bookstore on North Avenue. The people who listened to my story were very nice and laughed in the right places. To thank me for coming, Quimby's gave me a voucher good to buy something in the store.

I bought two copies of *Angry Teen Comics*.

Diary of a 2004 Congressional Candidate

Friday, May 7

This evening, the Florida Division of Elections website posted the names of all the qualifying candidates for Congress. I am one of three candidates in the Fourth Congressional District in the Jacksonville area.

Ander Crenshaw, the conservative Republican incumbent, faces a primary challenge from Deborah Katz Pueschel, who thinks he isn't right-wing enough to reverse what she calls our "current course of gradual socialism." Two years ago, Crenshaw beat her with 90 percent of the vote, and he's sure to win the G.O.P. nomination again.

I'm the only registered Democrat in the race. But, unable to afford the nine-thousand-dollar filing fee to get the official party designation, I'm a write-in candidate. Under Florida's bizarre election laws, write-in votes count only if they're for "qualified" candidates like me.

If I weren't a candidate, Congressman Crenshaw's name wouldn't be on the November ballot. There just wouldn't be an election. Four of Florida's twenty-five House members were elected this afternoon when they did not get a primary or write-in opponent.

Over 90 percent of Americans live in congressional districts that are essentially one-party monopolies. Of Florida's twenty-five House seats, seven are safe for Democrats, and sixteen are safe for Republicans.

The Fourth is the most Republican district in the state. But I'm hoping to give anyone opposed to Crenshaw's positions a chance to vote for someone else.

In the last Congress, Crenshaw voted for more Bush tax cuts and the war in Iraq. He supported oil development in the Arctic National Wildlife Refuge, limiting the Patients' Bill of Rights, and banning "partial-birth" abortion. Crenshaw voted against campaign-finance reform.

As of March, his campaign committee had $612,691 in cash.

Mine had bupkis.

- - - -

Saturday, May 8

When I was out last night, I got a phone message from a Pueschel supporter who wanted to know how much Rep. Crenshaw had paid me to "close" the Republican primary.

In Florida, everyone, regardless of party affiliation, can vote in a primary when only one party is running candidates for a particular office. But as a write-in candidate, I've created at least theoretical competition in November, so now Democrats and independents can't vote in the Republican primary.

Given that Pueschel is even further to the right than Crenshaw, I can't imagine why the caller thought she'd do better in a primary that included Democratic voters.

Besides, the Congressman would never pay someone like me to manipulate the election. As a candidate in the 1994 G.O.P. gubernatorial primary—in which he finished fourth—Crenshaw publicly vowed that he would never hire anyone who was gay.

- - - -

Monday, May 10

This morning the *Florida Times-Union'*s "Political Ticker" column listed my name with other candidates. The item said all five local members of Congress were sure bets for reelection. It noted that Rep. Corinne Brown, the Democrat whose district includes all of Jacksonville's nonwhite neighborhoods, is facing two "virtual unknowns" named Prince Brown and Johnny Brown.

I've run twice before as a write-in candidate against Republican House members, and experience tells me that press coverage can make a big difference.

In 1994, when I ran against Rep. Michael Bilirakis of Clearwater, the *Tampa Tribune* published a story about me on the front page of the local-news section. An African-American newspaper noticed I supported reparations for slavery and endorsed me. I got 153 votes.

Two years later, as the sole opponent of Rep. Ileana Ros-Lehtinen of Miami, I got no publicity and only eight write-in votes.

- - - -

Thursday, May 13

Today I got my first survey from a lobbying group.

Surveys from interest groups are fun to fill out and can help the campaign. Answering a survey from the National Organization for Women actually got me their endorsement in 1994.

This group is Gun Owners of America. Their letterhead says "27 Years of No Compromise—1975-2002," leading me to wonder if they started compromising last year or simply have not had a chance to update their stationery.

The letter, from John Velleco, the director of federal affairs for the Virginia-based organization, begins, "The members of Gun Owners of America in your state are extremely interested in your views on the subject of gun control."

The GOA 2004 Congressional Candidate Survey is four pages. My name, address, state, and congressional district are preprinted on the top of the first page. I must fill out, sign, and return the survey by May 31.

There are twelve questions, most with multiple parts. They've worded it so that a "Yes" response is their position, leading to questions asking if I would ...

... oppose requiring handgun buyers to pass a mandatory safety test?

... oppose requiring mandatory trigger locks or other locked-storage requirements?

... support a repeal of the 1993 Brady instant check?

... oppose legislation to keep in place the 1994 law banning many types of semiautomatic firearms and limiting magazine capacity?

I checked "No" on every question but one, and I think that was only because I misinterpreted it.

I answered "Yes" to number nine: "Would you oppose a ban on any type of ammunition?"

The follow-up question was: "If no, what type(s)?"

This confused me totally. I assumed they meant "If yes, what type(s)?" and in the space provided, I wrote, "BB gun pellets."

That won't be good enough to get me the endorsement of Gun Owners of America.

- - - -

Monday, May 17

A woman from Oklahoma named Tammy calls to tell me how I can use "voice-message marketing" in my campaign. She's gotten my number from the Florida Division of Elections website.

"By using our service," Tammy tells me, "you can send your personalized recorded message to home answering machines and what we call real people."

I could also do phone surveys and get real people to donate money.

"We give you a code to call into and our computer records your message and then dials the numbers of voters," Tammy says. "It will sound just like you would sound on the telephone, not like some computer-generated recording."

"So it's not a computer-generated recording?" I ask her.

"No, it is, but it doesn't sound like it," she says. "It sounds as if you're actually taking the time to call. Arnold Schwarzenegger called three million people this way. Some people were so excited by his call that they saved his messages—though I'm not sure what they'll do with them."

I point out that Arnold Schwarzenegger is a celebrity and nobody in Florida's Fourth Congressional District knows who I am. They won't recognize my high-pitched nasal New York accent and will hang up on me.

Then I remember that my brother Jonathan does a great Ah-nold imitation. Maybe I could have Jonathan record a message in Schwarzenegger's voice telling voters what a fahn-tas-tic candidate I am.

Tammy thinks this is a very creative idea. Her firm, MP Marketing, has been doing political campaigns for about a year. Mostly they do "commercial," meaning calls for satellite-TV companies trolling for subscribers, or doctors' offices doing collections or confirming appointments.

I tell Tammy it will be a while before I'd do any voice-message marketing. She says she'll send me the quotes on what five thousand calls would cost.

Before I hang up, I can't resist: "Hey, you're actually a person talking to me in real time, right?"

Tammy laughs. "That's what the voters in your district will think," she says.

- - - -

Tuesday, May 18

I find a letter from the Florida Department of State in my mailbox.

The Department of State contains both the Elections Division and the Cultural Affairs Division, so till I open the envelope, I'm not sure if it's related to my campaign or to my recent application for an individual-artist fellowship in fiction writing.

A week after the November 2000 presidential election, when former Secretary of State Katherine Harris was busy fixing things so that George W. Bush would win, she still had time to send out a letter nominating me to the Cultural Affairs Division's grant panel in multidisciplinary arts.

Today's letter, though, is from the Elections Division: a memo from Phyllis Hampton, the chief of the Bureau of Election Records.

She says that because my papers to qualify as a federal candidate are in order, under Section 101.5612

Florida Statutes, she is notifying me that voting equipment to be used in each county must be pretested prior to an election. I have the right to be present at the equipment pretest.

Florida's infamous punch cards and hanging chads from 2000—when nearly twenty-seven thousand votes for president were invalidated in Jacksonville—are now history.

We'll be voting with optical scanning and electronic touch-screen machines, which may be even worse, because they don't leave a paper trail.

In Duval County—Jacksonville—the Republican supervisor of elections has bought voting machines manufactured by Diebold, a company whose CEO, an important G.O.P. fundraiser, last year signed a letter pledging his commitment "to helping Ohio deliver its electoral votes to the President."

Diebold electronic voting machines were banned in four counties in California last month after vote counts malfunctioned. When the Diebold source code was accidentally posted online last year, computer scientists determined that it could easily be hacked to produce election fraud.

In Broward and Palm Beach last January, my friend Ellyn—one of the few intelligent Republicans I know—won a special election for the state legislature by just twelve votes. Electronic voting machines showed that 137 people who went to the polls cast no ballot, even though it was the day's only election.

Last month, the Elections Division ruled that it would not permit manual re-counts on touch-screen machines.

I would love to see how these new machines handle write-in votes.

- - - -

Wednesday, May 19

A week ago I wrote to *Folio Weekly*, Jacksonville's alternative newspaper, telling them about my campaign. Last night I got a message from a staff writer who wants to do a phone interview.

Before I call back, I Google him and find out he's into environmentalism and hip-hop. Doing background research on a journalist sort of makes me feel like a smarmy politician, but I guess I'd better get used to it.

The first thing the reporter wants to know is why I'm running in a congressional district in North Florida when I live in South Florida.

I explain that I was looking for a district in which no Democrat had filed against a Republican incumbent. Originally, I was going to run against Rep. Tom Feeney in Daytona Beach, but I got faked out by a report that a real Democrat was going to run in that district. Nobody did, and Feeney—more of a religious-right conservative than Crenshaw, the guy I'm running against—has already been re-elected without opposition.

I tell the reporter that I know Jacksonville from once teaching a college class that met on Saturday in the

9

phone-company building downtown. The course was called The Individual and Society. I had the students read Tocqueville and watch the movie *Ordinary People*.

The reporter asks what kind of people I think will vote for me.

"Since I'm a write-in candidate," I say, "they'll have to be able to write. So that basically lets out the entire population of Lake City."

I talk about my opposition to the war, about my going to demonstrations carrying a sign that said "Fifty Million Frenchmen Can't Be Wrong."

"Let's cut and run," I say, "and bring our torturers home."

The reporter laughs, but I remind myself to go easy on the jokes.

He asks my position on abortion rights (yes), the legalization of drugs (yes), and gay marriage (yes).

I say my campaign theme song is "Don't Believe the Hype" although I recognize that "Fight the Power" is the more obvious choice.

When I tell the reporter that the number of votes I get depends on how much media attention I get, he says, "Well, let's see if we can give you some publicity."

The article should be out next week, but since I'm not in Jacksonville, I'm relying on the paper to send me a copy.

I mail the reporter a stamped, self-addressed envelope, using the last of my Paul Robeson stamps.

- - - -

Thursday, May 20

The photo editor of *Folio Weekly* e-mails me. The paper needs a photo for the article, and the ones on my website are too small. They are also from 1999 and don't show how decrepit I actually am.

So I go to a local photography shop—their sign says "WEDDING PHOTOGRAPHY"—to get a quick headshot.

I'm wearing a dark T-shirt. At home beforehand, trying on various outfits, I was horrified to discover that in a tie and jacket, I look like I actually could be someone's congressman.

The photographers, two brothers in their mid-50s, tell me how good the picture will come out.

"How good could it possibly be?" I say. "You're starting out with a *meeskite*."

"Oh, he speaks Chinese," one brother says to the other.

It turns out they grew up in the Glenwood projects a few blocks from me in Brooklyn that we all went to J.H.S. 285. Too bad they don't live in the Fourth

Congressional District. I suspect few people from Brooklyn do.

As the younger brother takes my picture, he asks why the newspaper is doing a story on me.

"Oh, I'm a writer," I tell him. I'm too embarrassed to say I'm running for Congress.

I make sure he digitally fixes my turkey neck and softens my wrinkles before we e-mail the photo to *Folio Weekly* in Jacksonville.

- - - -

Monday, May 24

I get a postcard from VictoryStore.com, one of the many businesses that make money off political campaigns. They sell bumper stickers, posters, notepads, refrigerator magnets, and other tchotchkes. They do direct mail, automated phone calls (voice-message marketing?), polling, website design, signs, and banners.

VictoryStore.com campaign packages come in three sizes, ranging from $1699 to $599. Their Medium Campaign Package includes: 500 bumper stickers, 250 lawn/yard signs, 250 sign frames or wires, 1000 literature bags, 1000 lapel stickers, 24 campaign T-shirts, a 2-foot-by-6-foot banner, and a digital version of the *Winning the Tough Ones* campaign manual.

- - - -

Wednesday, May 26

I get a letter from John Berthoud, president of the National Taxpayers Union (NTU), asking me to fill out their 2004 Congressional Candidate Survey.

The Virginia-based organization plans to post my answers online "for the benefit of our 350,000-plus members."

"If you choose **not** to respond, you will be listed as *refused to respond* **or** *did not respond*," Berthoud writes. "We hope that you will respond because we want to be fair to you and every other candidate for the U.S. House or Senate."

NTU's affiliated PAC, the National Taxpayers Union Campaign Fund, "may well review" the surveys to determine endorsements.

I check their website and am kind of surprised to see that they've rated most of Florida's Republican House members, including Crenshaw, only a C+ on taxing and spending issues. Two ultraconservative GOP congressmen rate an A and get a Taxpayers' Friend Award. All the Florida Democrats get D or F. They are in NTU's "Big Spender" category, which is where I'd probably feel at home.

I check "No" to all 11 questions on the survey. I oppose tax limitation and balanced-budget amendments to the Constitution, "Social Security Choice," and repealing the entire federal tax code and replacing it with a national sales tax or "a single, low, flat-rate income tax."

I won't pledge to make all of Bush's tax cuts permanent or to ensure that legislation I sponsor will cause a net reduction in federal spending.

Finally, I sign my name under the sentence "My answers are a firm and unconditional commitment to the people of the United States" and send the questionnaire back to the National Taxpayers Union.

- - - -

Saturday, May 29

I came home from a day at the annual Memorial Day Hip-Hop Festival in Miami Beach to find the copy of the *Folio Weekly* article sent by the reporter, Hamilton Nolan.

It's titled "The Player," with the subhead "Congressional candidate Richard Grayson turns the political arena into a theatre of the absurd."

My photo is above Congressman Crenshaw's and is about three times the size of his picture.

The article begins: "Ander Crenshaw, the two-term Republican congressman from Florida's fourth district, is in for the fight of his life in the upcoming election ... If Crenshaw is to survive to see a third term in the U.S. House of Representatives, he will have to defeat a man whose name is recognized by literally dozens of Americans—Richard Grayson."

I'm called "every seasoned politician's worst fear—a verbose, unknown, unrestrained, write-in mock-challenger."

Nolan has used my joke about people in Lake City not being able to write and mentions that I find "particularly irksome" Crenshaw's remark that he would not knowingly hire a homosexual:

"In the unlikely event of a debate, Grayson says he would inquire whether the congressman 'is as stupid as that remark made him sound.' Crenshaw's office did not return a call seeking comment on the subject."

Other excerpts:

"Admittedly, Grayson's campaign isn't blasting into high gear. He says he makes an effort to do one campaign-oriented thing every day. On a recent afternoon, he selected his personal theme song: 'Don't Believe the Hype,' by Public Enemy. He briefly considered using 'Fight the Power,' but dismissed it as 'too trite.'"

"Grayson is chock-full of new ideas for the new century. He favors the decriminalization of marijuana, socialized health care and a speedy exit from the quagmire in Iraq. The focus, he says, should be on 'bringing our torturers home.'"

"Grayson lives in South Florida, and the distance has precluded him from scheduling any rallies in District 4. He says that he doesn't travel in the area much, but calls Jacksonville 'pretty cool,' having come a long way from its grimy, polluted past. 'I do notice the district is smelling better,' he says."

"He hopes to gain support from the vocal anti-Dubya demographic: 'I'm gonna get the people who hate

15

Bush,' he says, 'who want to see him as the guest of honor at a Fallujah barbecue.'"

"But perhaps Grayson is just the man for the job," the article ends. "'If you want to piss off the people at the Division of Elections, that's a good thing to do,' he says. "It's not gonna make a difference, but it might make you feel better.'"

Hamilton Nolan and *Folio Weekly* have provided the first real publicity for my campaign. I just hope it's not my last.

- - - -

Monday, June 28

I'm trying to catch up on the congressional-candidate questionnaires I've gotten while I was in Los Angeles the last few weeks.

Most of them follow the same format, largely yes/no questions, with "Yes" being the answer the organization doing the asking wants to hear.

The longest survey comes from Phyllis Schafly's right-wing Eagle Forum, with a checklist of 69, count 'em, 69 questions.

I find myself checking "No" after "No" to questions like these:

"Will you vote to abolish the National Endowment for the Arts?"

"Will you vote to defund the Violence Against Women Act, widely known as 'feminist pork'?"

"Will you vote to stop coed basic training in the Army, Navy, and Air Force?"

"Do you oppose the judge-invented notion that abortion is a right protected by the Constitution?"

After about 40 of these, I think, *Oh hell, I'll just check "No" all the way through.*

That's what I did on the eight-question "Freedom Survey" from Citizens for a Sound Economy, refusing to give my support to "class action lawsuit reform that ends frivolous lawsuits and returns our legal system to decent, honest Americans with real grievances" and "medical malpractice reform that will stop the fleecing of doctors, businesses, and consumers."

But then the Eagle Forum asks this question:

"Will you oppose any legislation that would make workforce training the mission of the schools?"

This stumps me. Having been a college teacher and administrator for nearly 30 years, I deplore the way higher education has increasingly emphasized the training of future corporate employees over learning for learning's sake.

Feeling I somehow must have misunderstood the question, I reluctantly check "Yes"—only to find myself in agreement with Eagle Forum on the next half-dozen other questions, including:

"Will you vote against any bill that preempts stronger state privacy laws?"

"Will you vote to prohibit the use of genetic testing as a condition for insurance coverage?"

"Will you oppose a National Constitutional Convention for any purpose?"

Agreement stops when I come to the penultimate question:

"Will you support withdrawing jurisdiction of the federal courts over challenges to the Defense of Marriage Act?"

Then a follow-up, the only question calling for a narrative answer:

"What *else* will you do to support traditional marriage?"

This stumps me for a while.

Finally, I scribble: "Kill Liza Minelli."

- - - -

Tuesday, June 29

The briefest and most puzzling questionnaire is the "Kids in Focus 2004 Candidate Survey" from the Vision Council of America.

The first four questions test my knowledge, asking stuff like "Did you know that undiagnosed vision

18

problems can lead to permanent vision loss and difficulty in school?"

The fifth and final question is this toughie:

"If elected, will you support increasing the number of children that receive an eye exam from an eye doctor?"

Who could be against *that*? A politician whose district's biggest employers are manufacturers of white canes?

In addition to the support/oppose checklists, sometimes surveys ask open-ended questions. *Por ejemplo*, Citizens for Global Solutions gives me two lines to write an answer to:

"What are the most important global problems facing the United States? How should the U.S. empower international organizations to address these concerns?"

I can fit in only 17 words about "empire" and cooperating with various international organizations, an answer whose banality nauseates me even as I squish in its last word, "peace," on the margin of the page.

Some of the surveys quiz me on issues that require me to do a lot of research to answer them—part of the fun of being a candidate. The Armenian National Committee of America's questions, for instance, include:

"Do you support maintaining Section 907 of the Freedom Support Act as a statement of U.S. opposition to Azerbaijan's blockades?"

After about half an hour of going through news articles, mostly from the BBC, I decide I do.

The Armenian survey made me think about issues that tend not to come up in conversations with even my most political of friends: stuff like Nagorno-Karabagh's right to self-determination and taxpayer subsidies for the Baku-Ceyhan pipeline route.

I tell the ANCA that I'm with Foreign Minister Oskanyan on these issues.

On the other hand, among the many international agreements the Bush administration hates, it's hard to give Citizens for Global Solutions my "three highest priorities for ratification."

I pick the Kyoto Protocol (climate change), the Ottawa Treaty (land mines), and the Vienna Convention on the Law of Treaties Between States and International Organizations or Between International Organizations.

It would be nice to be able to take congressional junkets to those cities, too.

- - - -

Sunday, July 4

I celebrate a glorious Fourth by filling out my July quarterly report for the Federal Election Commission. The FEC was established in the wake of the Watergate scandal, and as we all know, it has eliminated the corrupt influence of money on federal campaigns.

This report covers the period from April Fools' Day to June 30 and must be filed by all principal campaign committees of congressional candidates, including those who are unopposed and candidates whose names do not appear on the ballot—like me.

My principal campaign committee is called Democrat Grayson for the House and has been given the FEC identification number C00387829.

As the treasurer of the committee, I am the custodian of records and am responsible for filling out a summary and then a detailed statement of our contributions and expenditures. Since my campaign took in no money during April, May, or June, this mostly involves entering zeros in lots of little boxes.

I do not have to fill out FEC Form 3's Schedule D: Debts and Obligations, as I owe no money to fat cats or thin dogs.

As for FEC Form 3Z-1, which is titled—I do not kid—Consolidated Report of Gross Receipts for Authorized Committees (Millionaires' Amendment), the less said, the better.

- - - -

Tuesday, July 13

Every day now I get mail from companies that make money off political candidates. Some examples:

1. A video titled *Reach the People and Win*, from Duplication Factory, CD/video marketing specialists, that tells me, "Many politicians are still making the mistake of

21

giving only 'the facts' and missing the emotional element that video can provide."

2. A postcard from Mid State Screen Graphics, trying to sell me a sign printed on Colorplast™ corrugated plastic, "the most weatherproof and durable sign material you can use in Florida's sunny/windy/rainy/hot/humid environment."

3. A packet from Magnet Street, with samples showing me how I can increase my name recognition as a candidate by placing magnets with my name on them inside voters' homes.

4. A letter from Imprint Promotions that begins, "Dear Richard, I know you are busy, I will make this quick. First, I wanted to thank you for your commitment to making our nation a better place," before going on to tell me about the bumper stickers, buttons, and banners I can purchase from them.

5. A leaflet from *The Almanac of Federal PACs: 2004-05*, a volume that contains contacts for every political action committee that contributed at least $25,000 to candidates in the 2002 election. ("When you're hunting for PAC money, it helps to have a map!")

6. A brochure from Outdoor Mobile Media touting their billboards as the best way of "maximizing those 2.3 seconds you've got to reach those undecided voters!"

7. A letter from Fiberhaus Consulting ("Value. Empathy. Passion. Interaction.") telling me about PoliticalAssist, a line of software that will reduce time spent on such activities as volunteer training, data entry, and voter outreach by 40 percent. Its CodeFleet program enables

campaign workers to "immediately record results from volunteers who make personal contact with voters using bar codes and scanners."

- - - -

Wednesday, July 14

Last night I threw out all my candidate junk mail but couldn't bear to give up my favorite: the glossy catalog from Donahue Campaign & Election Products, featuring a cornucopia of useful merchandise.

They offer items like a 7-foot-by-10-foot hot-air balloon with my slogan on it for $650 and a fan printed in red and blue on white six-ply cardboard, coated on one side. The illustration fan says, "I'm a Fan of Shelly Kelb Price for Webster County Clerk."

Donahue's biggest seller is "The Winningest Sign," available "in brilliant colors and featuring a no-show-thru material, totally weatherproof, printed both sides with non-fading ink." A thousand of these Winningest signs in two colors, 26 feet by 16 feet, would set me back $1942. Eager for bipartisan sales, Donahue illustrates this item with samples that say "Bush/Cheney" and "Tom Daschle for South Dakota."

I can also buy custom-design litterbags (1000 for $155); book matches with my logo ($90 for one case); rulers and yardsticks; "fun flyers" (Frisbee must be a trademark); suede coasters; super-soaker sponges ("Rise Up and Elect McLin State Senator"); seed packets ("Sow the Seeds of Victory for Keith for Circuit Judge"); golf tees; wooden nickels; sewing kits; unbreakable plasti-clip ad-combs; emery boards; fly swatters; magic-grip jar openers; doorknob hangers; and fortune cookies.

Another item on sale is a bookmark featuring my campaign slogan and my choice of a calendar, a list of the Presidents, or the Serenity Prayer, 500 for $135.

God grant me the PAC contributions to pay for all this stuff.

- - - -

Friday, July 16

Today I get a letter that I'm too scared to open for a while. It's from the Department of Defense. The last piece of mail I got bearing that return address traumatized me.

That 1970 letter carried the salutation "Greetings!" It invited me to spend several hours at Fort Hamilton walking around in my underwear with 100 other 18-year-olds to be assessed for my fitness to serve as cannon fodder in Vietnam.

To my relief, today's invitation will not require getting notes from psychiatrists about the guarded prognosis of my extremely serious mental illness.

(When candidate-information forms include a space for my military experience, I write in "Draft Dodger.")

Pursuant to the Uniformed and Overseas Citizens Absentee Voting Act (UOCAVA), the Defense Department is giving 2004 congressional candidates the opportunity to record a personal audio message to all military personnel, their family members, and U.S. citizens residing overseas.

The Pentagon's Voting Information Center advises me to keep my recorded message short because "callers tend to switch to another message after about one minute."

Vowing to control my tendency to ramble, I call their number in Northern Virginia. ("Collect calls are not accepted.")

As suggested, I open by introducing myself:

"Hey, I'm Richard Grayson, a liberal Democrat running for Congress from Florida's Fourth District."

I spell my name and give the URL for my website. ("You may also give contact information should the caller want to find out more about your platform.")

Another bit of advice from the DOD: "Keep in mind that over half the callers are in the military; however, they are as interested in all timely issues as locals are."

It's always good to stick to three issues. I will tell them I'm against the war in Iraq, and if they don't hang up after that, they'll hear me say I'm for socialized medicine ... and then ... I get stuck on the third issue.

I don't know whether to pick raising the minimum wage, protecting the environment, or other issues like education, civil liberties, or the budget deficit. How specific can I be in seven seconds?

Finally, I lamely come out in favor of "equal rights for all Americans" but don't have time to add "regardless of race, gender, sexual orientation, marital status, religion, disability, or national origin."

After listening to my just-recorded message to military voters, I'm really happy that I haven't yet been interviewed on the radio.

- - - -

Saturday, July 17

For a second time, I send my candidate questionnaire to the Florida National Organization for Women's Political Action Committee.

Linda Miklowitz, their president, called to say she mislaid my first e-mailed questionnaire. Their endorsement meeting in Orlando is coming up and she didn't want me "to get left out."

Rep. Crenshaw is anti-choice and generally terrible on women's issues. I know my positions are pretty much what FL-NOW-PAC supports.

I'm in favor of an equal-rights amendment, affirmative action, government funding of abortions, marriage equality, campaign-finance reform, and universal health care.

But when they asked if I had a campaign plan, I had to write: "Not really."

Their final question was open-ended:

"Define 'feminist.'"

As an undergrad, I took a Sex and Politics seminar and read a lot of feminist theory. I read more in a law-school Feminist Jurisprudence class.

I wrote that I'm not smart enough to give a good definition. Then I relied on the old Potter Stewart dodge:

"But I do know a feminist when I see one, and I see one in the mirror every morning when I'm shaving."

- - - -

Sunday, July 18

Googling, I discover that Café Press—the website where I bought my "Punks for Dean" T-shirt and my "Pardon Martha!" coffee mug—is selling a red and blue bumper sticker that says "Grayson / U.S. Congress."

Product Number 11930389 sells for $3.95, measures "a generous 10 x 3 inches," and is printed on 4-mil. vinyl so it will neither fade in the sun nor bleed in the rain.

The product copy says: "Richard Grayson is definitely one of the more irregular congressional candidates there is, running against Bush/Cheney Republican Ander Crenshaw. Grayson is a write in candidate, so give him your vote."

I click on their page for Florida campaign stuff and I see my bumper sticker is fourth, just after the John Kerry Florida Fleece Shorts, the Florida Democratic Coffee Mug, and the Florida John Kerry Baseball Cap,

27

and before bumper stickers for Corinne Brown and Allan Boyd, who are actual members of Congress.

The last item is a bumper sticker reading "Florida Says Vote Kucinich."

I order three Grayson bumper stickers for myself and click on "Tell a friend about this product!"

Later, my father calls from Arizona to say he's buying one, too.

Neither of us will actually put it on the back of our cars.

I want my 2000 Chevy Cavalier to be bumper-sticker-free in case one day I have to sell it to a conservative.

- - - -

Friday, July 23

Yesterday, the House passed the Marriage Protection Act. This bill strips federal courts of jurisdiction over the Defense of Marriage Act, a 1996 law saying that states need not recognize same-sex-union laws of other states.

In other words, Congress is saying it should be able to pass a law and prevent courts from even *considering* the law's constitutionality.

Rep. Crenshaw, like most Republicans, voted for this ludicrous bill.

Thirty-five years ago, Crenshaw graduated from the University of Florida law school.

Ten years ago, I graduated from the same school with high honors. I'm sure Constitutional Law has always been a required course.

Crenshaw must have read *Marbury v. Madison*, the 1803 ruling establishing judicial review. He should know the Supreme Court is the final authority on a law's constitutionality.

I actually first learned about *Marbury v. Madison* and separation of powers back in junior high.

So what was Crenshaw doing at UF? Well, I've heard he founded a chapter of Campus Crusade for Christ and courted his wife Kitty there. Back then, Kitty's father, Claude Kirk, was the Republican governor.

Kirk was a flamboyant figure, a kind of Floridian Huey Long. At his inaugural ball, the divorced governor introduced his stunning young fiancée only as "Madame X." A populist, Kirk shook up a sleepy Southern state.

In 1988, I voted for Kirk, who had switched parties, in the Democratic Senate primary. He finished fifth, with 5 percent of the vote. "It's lonely here at the bottom," Kirk said.

At Alabama Law School, Kirk said, he never got above a C.

But I bet Kirk knows that the courts will declare the Marriage Protection Act unconstitutional. I bet his son-in-law knows it, too.

Of course, Congress could always pass a Marriage Protection Act Protection Act to try to prevent that. And a Marriage Protection Act Protection Act Protection Act after that.

My head hurts to think about it.

- - - -

Tuesday, July 27

The League of Women Voters of Tallahassee has invited me to participate in some campaign events they are sponsoring. Among them is "Bandwagon 2004," to take place at the WFSU public-TV studio on Red Barber Plaza.

"Bandwagon 2004" will be a live TV show that will give candidates for Congress, county commissioner, sheriff, tax collector, property appraiser, and Ochlockonee River Soil & Water Conservation Supervisor the opportunity to have two minutes of airtime.

The letter says, "The Bandwagon 2004 atmosphere again will be that of an old-fashioned political rally complete with lively music such as that of John Philip Sousa or a barbershop quartet when your two minutes are up. You are encouraged to bring supporters (no more than 10 per candidate) carrying campaign signs. These supporters and the signs may appear on television, too."

The Fourth Congressional District is so weirdly drawn to include the maximum number of GOP voters that it extends over 160 miles from its heart in

Jacksonville to take in a Republican sliver of Florida's capital city.

Tallahassee is a great town, but it's a nine-hour drive from my house—too far to go for two minutes on TV.

- - - -

Friday, July 30

Yesterday, I got a notice to pick up a certified letter at the post office. It turns out to be from the Christian Coalition of Florida, asking me to fill out their candidate-issues survey.

These questionnaires are coming in at the rate of about one a day now. This must be religious week, as I got one a few days ago from Joyce Meyers Ministries.

At first I was impressed, because Joyce Meyers Ministries' questions were worded so neutrally that I couldn't tell they were typical right-wing nuts till I checked their website. Then I realized that Joyce Meyers Ministries must maintain a façade of nonpartisanship to keep their tax exemption as a religious organization.

The Christian Coalition survey lists 97 issues. Next to each one, I must draw a circle around the appropriate letter: "S"=Support, "O"=Oppose, "U"=Undecided.

It also has spaces for me to fill in my pastor's name and my church. I write "None" in both those spaces. I'm an atheist.

But given the state of my campaign, I'm thinking about offering a novena to St. Jude, patron saint of hopeless causes.

- - - -

Saturday, July 31

The survey in this morning's mail comes not from a religious group but from the Florida Music Educators' Association. While Crenshaw wants to sharply cut arts funding, I support the FMEA's positions on strengthening the fine-arts curriculum in the schools.

Their final question:

"What cultural events (concerts, exhibitions, etc.) have you attended in the past year?"

I jot down a few, and then write:

"I don't have space or time to list all of them. Right now I'm on my way to the Pompano Beach Amphitheater for the Warped Tour, where I will encourage the children in the mosh pit to appreciate fine music."

I hope the fine music includes Taking Back Sunday's "You're So Last Summer." That song should be taught in every school in this state.

- - - -

Sunday, August 1

I meet my friends Alex and Luis for lunch at Stork's Bakery, which is owned by another congressional candidate running against a Republican incumbent.

Jim Stork, the former mayor of Wilton Manors, is a longtime gay and community activist. He's trying to unseat Clay Shaw, who's represented the Fort Lauderdale area in the House for over 20 years.

Stork has the endorsement of many liberal organizations. Alex and Luis want to know why I don't try to get similar support.

I explain that these groups don't want to endorse hopeless candidates. It doesn't look good to prospective contributors if they support well-meaning losers.

For example, even though Ander Crenshaw has a zero percent rating on gay and lesbian issues from the Human Rights Campaign, I have no chance for their backing.

As their website states, "The organization does not make an endorsement in a situation where the candidate has no chance of getting elected but is supportive of HRC issues ... This serves to maintain the value of HRC's endorsement by not watering down the respected reputation of the organization by endorsing anyone regardless of his or her viability."

Similarly, the Gay and Lesbian Victory Fund supports gay candidates who have a chance to win. They especially love endorsing people who are shoo-ins, because that makes their track record look better.

Candidates seeking Victory Fund endorsement have to answer questions I couldn't answer in a million years, like these:

"Describe your fundraising plan. How much have you raised to date and from what sources? How will you raise the rest of your budget? Include a breakout by categories such as major donors, individuals, PACs, corporations, direct mail, house parties, etc. How much cash do you have on hand?"

"What consultants have been hired for media, polling and/or fundraising? Please describe their background, experience and extent of their relationship to your campaign."

Jim Stork—bakery owner, former mayor, successful fundraiser—can answer these questions. He's got lots of support, and more importantly, a real chance to win in a competitive district and become Florida's first openly gay Democratic Congressman. (A semi-openly gay Republican currently represents the Palm Beach area.)

So when my friends offer to write out a small check for my campaign, I tell them to instead give their money to a viable politician like Stork.

"We just did," Alex says, pointing to the few crumbs left on their plates from the beef-and-raisin empanadas they had for lunch.

- - - -

Saturday, August 7

I check out the website of Citizens for a Sound Economy, former House Majority Leader Dick Armey's PAC, whose Freedom Survey I answered weeks ago.

Since that time, Citizens for a Sound Economy has merged with Empower America to form FreedomWorks. I suppose this is the political equivalent of ExxonMobil, except that FreedomWorks won't be underwriting any shows on PBS.

FreedomWorks has posted my responses to the survey. I am the only congressional candidate in Florida who has responded "No" to supporting all of the planks on their Freedom Agenda (flat tax, school vouchers, making Bush's tax cuts permanent).

Actually, I'm the only one who has responded "No" to more than a couple of questions. Most of the responders are Republicans who said "Yes" to everything.

But the other candidates in my district are listed as "Has not or refuses to respond."

There is a space for reader comments. I post mine:

"Richard Grayson of Davie, FL: 'As the Democratic candidate for the House in Florida's 4th Congressional District, I was happy to fill out this survey. Why have my Republican opponents, Deborah Katz Pueschel and Congressman Ander Crenshaw, refused to respond? Are they enemies of Dick Armey?'"

I wonder how long they'll leave that up there.

- - - -

Wednesday, August 11

The hottest political issue for Jacksonville congressional candidates is apparently not the war or the economy but where to put a cemetery.

Every day, the *Florida Times-Union* seems to have another story about how Rep. Crenshaw is fighting to have a new national veterans' cemetery placed near Jacksonville International Airport.

Jacksonville's Democratic congresswoman, Corrine Brown, has joined Crenshaw in this battle against another Republican congressman, who wants the cemetery in his district south of Jacksonville.

Just a few weeks ago, Brown reprised her bravura performance in *Fahrenheit 9/11* and, on the House floor, charged that the GOP "stole" the 2000 presidential election by staging a "coup d'état." Crenshaw and other Republicans then voted to strike Brown's remarks from the record.

But Brown and Crenshaw are united in making sure dead veterans get buried in their hometown rather than in points south. They argue that the Jacksonville site would be more convenient for dead people in nearby southern Georgia.

This is the bread-and-butter stuff that members of Congress get elected on. All politics is yokel.

After considering this grave issue, I also support burying veterans near the airport.

People don't like to drive far to visit their deceased relatives. The Jacksonville site is much closer to the interstate.

- - - -

Thursday, August 19

I have gotten four identical e-mails from voters in the last couple of days. They each begin:

Dear,

As one of the American Heart Association's 22.5 million volunteers, I am concerned about the senseless deaths that continue to result from tobacco use.

These voters go on to ask me to support legislation that will give the Food and Drug Administration the power to regulate tobacco. I answer every one of these letters, pledging to do just that.

I try to reciprocate their affectionate salutation by addressing them variously as "Hon," "Sweetie," "Babe," and "Darling."

- - - -

Saturday, August 21

At its recent state-council meeting, the Florida National Organization for Women PAC made its endorsements of candidates.

Their highest level of support is "endorsement plus PAC contribution."

Second best is "endorsement."

After that comes "support." That is for "a candidate who is good on all of our issues but won't take a leadership role, or is good only on most of our issues but has a problem with one or two."

Florida NOW PAC did not endorse or support me.

However, they did "recommend" me.

That's a status reserved for "a candidate who is good on a few of our issues, but will not be a leader, or a candidate who is not very good on our issues but is significantly better than their opposition."

I'm not sure which category they put me in.

If Florida's feminists haven't embraced my campaign, they've sort of done what my great-aunts used to do when I was a kid: they've pinched me on the cheek.

- - - -

Tuesday, August 24

I was interviewed for two hours tonight at a nearby coffee bar by Trevor Aaronson, a reporter from Broward/Palm Beach *New Times*.

Trevor is about 24. I had to explain to him who Bella Abzug, John Anderson, and Mario Vargas Llosa were.

I've checked out Trevor's stories in Florida alternative weeklies. He manages to dig up dirt on most of the people he writes about.

For example, Trevor's article on Jim Stork, the Democratic candidate for Congress from Fort Lauderdale, emphasized Stork's involvement in questionable business dealings and an alleged death threat he made to an ex-boyfriend.

I wonder if those revelations have anything to do with Stork suspending his campaign, saying he was suffering from "fatigue."

Of course, a good scandal could only jump-start my own faltering campaign. So I brought along a bunch of clippings and other material on myself, hoping this will help Trevor uncover my sleazy past.

- - - -

Wednesday, August 25

This afternoon, John Anderson came down to my cubicle at work. Trevor had left a message on John's voice mail, asking him to comment on my candidacy.

Of course, John knew nothing about it, as I was too embarrassed to tell him. I am in awe of John, the only non-Democrat for whom I voted for president.

In 1980, disgusted with Carter and confronted with a Reagan landslide, I cast my ballot for John, a 10-term moderate Republican congressman from Illinois running as an independent.

Now over 80 and still incredibly vigorous, John is a law professor at the university where I work. In the past, I have talked to him about the dearth of competition in U.S. House districts.

John has written about last spring's U.S. Supreme Court opinion *Vieth v. Jubelirer*. By a 5-4 vote, the justices rejected a Democratic challenge to a Pennsylvania legislative plan that created bizarrely shaped computer-generated districts that maximized the number of Republican seats.

Writing for four members of the court, Justice Scalia said such cases should not even get into court, because no workable standards exist for deciding fairness in political redistricting. A fifth justice, Anthony Kennedy, said the complaint should be rejected but refused to say that a test for when a dominant party goes too far could never be devised.

But right now it looks as if there's no way to challenge the partisan gerrymandering that created our current uncompetitive congressional-district boundaries.

John and his co-author, Robert Richie, wrote in *Legal Times*:

"The lockdown of the U.S. House has major repercussions for representative government. Men continue to hold more than 85 percent of seats, and the number of African-Americans has decreased from its high. Leadership is essentially fixed, with partisan control of the House changing just once since 1954. Members are polarized, with very little compromise and negotiation across party lines."

John believes that we need "non-winner-take-all, multi-member district systems" to "fully and accurately represent the majority of voters."

Of course, all this seems pretty far removed from my rather silly little campaign, which I discuss with John for about 20 minutes.

He says he will call the reporter and tell him I am "a man of principle."

Right now I feel more like a man of stupidity.

- - - -

Friday, August 27

I find a *Florida Times-Union* article on the Fourth District GOP primary. It notes that an unnamed November write-in candidate keeps Democrats from voting this Tuesday.

The headline refers to Deborah Katz Pueschel, Rep. Crenshaw's opponent, as a "perennial candidate."

Pueschel ran against him in 2000 and 2002. Before that, she never ran for anything. So this is her third run for Congress, just as it is Crenshaw's.

Crenshaw has been a successful candidate for the state legislature six times.

And he ran unsuccessfully in Republican primaries for Florida secretary of state in 1978 and for governor in 1994.

So Crenshaw has run for office 11 times to Pueschel's three times. But she's the perennial candidate.

Pueschel's website, Quest for America, begins with a biblical reference:

As in my name sake, Deborah—'it has been said that women in politics must not look for honor or merely to have a voice in government. They must have devotion to a purpose. This Deborah had.'

And I too have devotion to a purpose in my passion to serve you.

On the website, I learn interesting facts about Deborah and her family. Her great-great-uncle, "Move-Up" Joe, played baseball with the 1887 New York Giants.

- - - -

Sunday, August 29

Today's *Times-Union* endorses Crenshaw, calling him "competent, capable and conservative."

The editorial also says he is "a good counterweight" to the "showboating" of Jacksonville's other House member, Corrine Brown.

After paragraphs excoriating her behavior and enumerating the ways "Jacksonville's national self-image has not been well served" by Congresswoman Brown's "frenetic" conduct, the editorial then says:

"On the other hand, she is a philosophical fit for the majority of voters in the district, which was designed to elect a liberal. Therefore, we recommend that she be nominated again."

Huh?

- - - -

Tuesday, August 31

Checking the primary results before I go to bed, I see that Crenshaw has beaten Pueschel by the exact same 90 percent-10 percent margin he did in 2002.

- - - -

Thursday, September 2

As Hurricane Frances approaches Florida, the media are telling residents to keep two things in mind:

1. There is no reason to panic.

2. We are all going to die.

I go out early to get a copy of this week's *New Times* and read Trevor Aaronson's piece on my campaign. Since my car has to wait in a gas-station line reminiscent of the Carter administration, I have plenty of time to count up the 13 factual errors in the 1,400-word article.

They range from my birthplace (the Bronx? No thonx!) and the wording of my bumper stickers to various errors in chronology and the address of my website.

While it would have been nice for one of my books to get a favorable *Miami Herald* review, I don't recall that happening. And I thought I had said I take antidepressants, not antipsychotic medicine.

But hey, I guess I'm so drugged up, I don't know what I'm talking about.

Nevertheless, Trevor Aaronson manages to create an image that is sure to help me on the campaign trail. Adjectives he uses to describe me include "cheap," "overanxious," "clumsy," "quirky," and "illogical."

I especially like this quote: "Grayson is a Renaissance man not because he's particularly brilliant but because he can't seem to stick to one thing."

But I'm a little worried about the article saying that John Anderson "has thrown his political weight behind the long shot."

John is quoted as saying of me, "He is an individual that some will dismiss as quixotic. Others will use less-kind adjectives ..."

The article ends by catching me in an unguarded moment, after I am asked what I would do if I were miraculously elected to Congress:

"I don't know where I'd live in Washington. I'd see if I could get a dorm room at American University. It *would* be interesting to be in Congress. But it's a lot of work. I'm too lazy to be in Congress."

I'd be worried about my candidacy self-destructing, but on the radio I hear there's now a hurricane warning and people in low-lying areas need to evacuate.

The talk-show host, Neil Rogers, says the way to tell if you live in a low-lying area is to look at your driver's license. If it says "Florida," then you live in low-lying area.

My campaign may be lying low for a while.

- - - -

Monday, September 6

I survived Hurricane Frances by moving into my windowless bathroom. I hadn't spent so much continuous time there since the night before my colonoscopy, but it was a nice break from politics.

Now that I have electricity again, I go online and find a *Florida Times-Union* headline: "Crenshaw to Help Others Campaign."

"Fresh off his easy primary election win," the article says, "U.S. Rep. Ander Crenshaw of Jacksonville said he intends to help 17 Republicans seeking to win House seats in tough races."

Crenshaw, the article says, "is expected to defeat write-in Richard Grayson in November."

"Defeat" doesn't sound so bad when I consider the alternative words the reporter might have chosen—such as "trounce," "rout," "crush," "annihilate," or "wipe the floor with."

- - - -

Wednesday, September 8

On his campaign website, Rep. Crenshaw has put up a letter to voters:

Dear Friends:

I am overwhelmed by the outpouring of support I received from my neighbors and friends in the Fourth Congressional District. As a result of your efforts, we received 90% of the vote on August 31st ...

I will remain steadfast in my support for the ideals that we share. Again, thank you for your overwhelming support and I look forward to continuing to represent the Fourth Congressional District of Florida.

Sincerely,

Ander

I wonder if he is even aware of my existence—the way, say, an elephant might be of a gnat that his tail has inadvertently swatted away.

His website features photos with these captions:

"Ander visits with local children and volunteers building a new playground."

"Ander addresses supporters at a campaign rally."

"Ander places signs."

There's one of him with the House GOP majority leader that should have this caption:

"Ander plays Fonzworth Bentley to Tom DeLay's P. Diddy."

If the people in the Kerry campaign are starting to panic, my own campaign needs about 10,000 milligrams of Ativan.

- - - -

Friday, September 10

A few weeks ago I filled out the National Political Awareness Test (NPAT), which is circulated every two years by Project Vote Smart, a nonpartisan organization.

The group has no political ideology other than disseminating standardized information on candidates to help the public be more informed at the polls.

The NPAT was the most extensive candidate survey I filled out.

Candidates must indicate, using a 1-6 numerical scale—with 1 as "greatly increase," 3 as "maintain status," 5 as "greatly decrease," and 6 as "eliminate"— what level of federal funding they support in two dozen general categories, such as military hardware, space-exploration programs, and national parks.

Using the same 1-6 scale, candidates have to say how they would deal with income taxes at various family-income levels and other taxes, tax deductions, and credits—for example, gasoline taxes or child tax credits.

Then candidates are supposed to check the principles they support in 14 issue categories. There are 13 principles under "Education Issues" alone, so the NPAT is pretty extensive.

Project Vote Smart has listed my complete NPAT answers on their website so voters can see that I favor eliminating federal funding for the "war on drugs," lifting the travel ban to Cuba, and prohibiting PAC contributions to federal candidates.

As for my opponent, Project Vote Smart has this notice, written in bright-red capital letters:

> *REPRESENTATIVE ANDER CRENSHAW HAS REFUSED TO PROVIDE ANY RESPONSES TO CITIZENS ON ISSUES THROUGH THE 2004 NATIONAL POLITICAL AWARENESS TEST. REPRESENTATIVE ANDER CRENSHAW REFUSED TO PROVIDE THIS INFORMATION WHEN ASKED TO DO SO ON 2 SEPARATE OCCASIONS BY:*
> *John McCain, Republican Senator*
> *Geraldine Ferraro, Former Democratic Congresswoman*
> *Michael Dukakis, Former Democratic Governor*
> *Bill Frenzel, Former Republican Congressman*
> *Richard Kimball, Project Vote Smart President*
> *THIS CANDIDATE WILL BE ASKED AGAIN TO PROVIDE RESPONSES DURING THE GENERAL ELECTION.*

Being a shoo-in for re-election in November means never having to fill out surveys.

- - - -

Sunday, September 12

I get a call from Jeremy, who says he's with the Florida State University Students United for Peace and Justice.

They're getting together a voter's guide and would like my positions on the issues. I wait for him to ask questions, but he wants it freeform.

I tell Jeremy I need to go to the other room and get my platform—my answers to the NPAT. I also ask him if he wants me to turn the music down so he can hear me better.

"No, it's really cool," Jeremy says. "What is it?"

I tell him it's Taking Back Sunday's new CD, *Where You Want to Be*.

Then I just happen to mention my plan to create a National Museum of Punk Culture on the Washington Mall.

"Awesome," Jeremy says.

To rev up my campaign, I've decided I need to start pandering.

- - - -

Thursday, September 16

I didn't pander enough to a group called Rescue American Jobs.

They gave me only 30 out of 100 points on my answers to their congressional-candidate survey.

I fared badly on questions like the one on foreign-guest-worker programs such as the H1-B visa that my friend Prabhdeep is here on. I wrote:

"They should be used only when genuine labor shortages occur."

Their comment:

"5 points for seemingly recognizing that these programs are overused. However, minus 25 points for not understanding that a labor shortage never occurs within a free market."

So I'm not Adam Smith. But at least I know where "only" should go in a sentence.

On the other hand, they gave me 4 out of 5 points on my final answer, my opinion of the corruption of the U.S. political system by corporate and foreign interests. I wrote:

"It sucks moose."

Rescue American Jobs' comment:

"One extra point for summing it up better than any other candidate."

- - - -

Saturday, September 18

Today I met an actual Fourth Congressional District voter.

Jeffrey, the 21-year-old cousin of a neighbor, is visiting from Jacksonville. Two weeks ago, Jeffrey came back from Iraq after serving there 16 months with his National Guard unit.

He was stationed in Kuwait, but his unit would take supplies up to northern Iraq every few weeks. He said the caravan got shot at, but nobody really was hurt bad. His only injury was to his knee, and that was from tripping over a carton of freeze-dried food.

I'm too embarrassed to mention my campaign for Congress, although Jeffrey is the first person I know who could actually vote for me. But he's a soldier, and I don't want to get into an argument with him about the war, which I figure he supports.

So I ask Jeffrey how the food over there was.

He says in Kuwait it was terrible, but at the Baghdad airport they had the best meals of his whole tour of duty.

Then his cousin says they've got to go.

As I'm shaking Jeffrey's hand goodbye, he suddenly blurts out, "Vote for Kerry, not for Bush," and runs off as if he's embarrassed for having said it.

Maybe I can get his address from his cousin to ask him to write me in.

- - - -

Monday, September 20

 More working-class people could run for Congress if they were not encumbered by full-time jobs.

 I work in an office from 8:30 a.m. to 5:00 p.m. every weekday. I sit in a cubicle, stare at a computer screen, and get yelled at a lot.

 Since my employer does not offer paid leave to political candidates, it's really hard for me to get up to Jacksonville to campaign. Besides, there's no one in my office to step in temporarily and get yelled at for me.

 So I can't make the Jacksonville Regional Chamber of Commerce's pre-election open-house "HobNob" despite the group's assurance that they will not charge me an attendance fee and their generous offer of an 8-foot table to display bumper stickers, yard signs, and "other collateral campaign material."

 Nor can I attend the Chets Creek Elementary School PTA's "Issues and Information Night," at which I'd be allotted five minutes to speak.

 It's my good fortune that these two events are scheduled for the same evening. By declining both invitations, I'm not favoring one group and alienating the other.

 State Farm Insurance writes that they too usually have a candidates' night.

But this year, "due to the need to take care of our policyholders affected by the hurricanes, we've decided to take a different tact [*sic*]."

They are having a Candidate Literature Fair in October and don't need my presence, just 200 pieces of my campaign literature.

Luckily, my office has a photocopy machine.

- - - -

Friday, September 24

At last, I get a full-fledged endorsement. And it's a complete surprise.

Drug WarRants based its 2004 Voters Guide on candidates' answers to the Project Vote Smart survey. They also looked at House members' votes on the Hinchey Amendment, which would stop federal-government interference with medical marijuana in states where it is legal.

Rep. Crenshaw twice voted against the Hinchey Amendment.

I support medical marijuana and oppose funding of the phony-baloney "war on drugs."

I also support decriminalizing possession of small amounts of marijuana, like the dime bags reportedly (according to Kitty Kelly's "sources") bought by that go-to girl, our nation's favorite ex-librarian.

There's a big red check next to my name on the Drug WarRants website, and it says:

"Grayson is a great choice here. He's smart and funny and has excellent views on the drug war. You'll like him. Vote for him."

If only I could get the AFL-CIO to smoke what Drug WarRants was smoking when they wrote that.

- - - -

Monday, September 27

I am finally going to set foot in the Fourth Congressional District.

Jacksonville's channel 47, a CBS affiliate, sent me a letter saying they "will provide five minutes of free air time, in prominent newscast time periods, to major candidates in selected races."

They have predetermined that I am major and selected.

I have to go to their studio for the taping.

The first four minutes will consist of responses to four questions solicited from their viewers and posed by a news anchor. The remaining minute will consist of "five quick questions ... designed to help viewers better understand you as a person."

The station reserves the right to edit the tape if the content of my answers does not adhere to "generally-accepted norms of propriety."

Eager for the free publicity and determined to be proper, I make reservations on Southwest to fly to Jacksonville and back. I'll be there for 24 hours.

- - - -

Wednesday, September 29

I get an e-mail from Debora, a professor who has lived in Germany for many years.

This year Debora registered to vote "with a purpose: to dump Bush."

Irritated to find that her ballot gave her the choice of Rep. Crenshaw or nothing, Debora Googled "write-in" and "District 4 Florida" and found me.

The lead story in today's *New York Times*, about the difficulties overseas voters face, contains this sentence:

"In Florida in 2000, late-arriving ballots became a divisive issue when some were counted and others were disqualified."

Debora says she mailed out her ballot today.

So if I don't get at least one vote, Debora will know for sure that her ballot wasn't counted.

- - - -

Saturday, October 2

I get a panic attack on the plane going to Jacksonville and another one when I get lost on my way to the TV studio. But finally I am in the Fourth Congressional District.

The part I'm in looks like a generic multicultural Sun Belt suburb. There are lots of Pentecostal and Baptist churches, but also a Baha'i temple. In strip malls I spot grocery stores called "Pinoy Market" and "Indo-Pak Mart" where Filipinos and South Asians can buy the food they like.

I drive behind several pickup trucks with Bush-Cheney stickers, but at the Publix supermarket where I'm buying my lunch—low-carb bagel, Smart Beat fake cheese slices, cut-up fruits and veggies—I meet two emo-looking young guys who tell me they're going to see Dashboard Confessional tonight at the nearby University of North Florida.

One of them is wearing a T-shirt that says "LOSER" and I think of buying it off him so I can wear it on TV instead of the dress shirt, tie, and sport jacket I've got on.

The woman ahead of me on the checkout line is wearing a burqa, with everything covered except her eyes and hands.

My sport jacket and shirt are black and my tie is pink because I don't want to look like a typical candidate. I've got on blue jeans and white sneakers because I figure I'll be sitting behind a desk.

I get to Clear Channel's office-park headquarters early for my 2:30 p.m. taping. Clear Channel owns the local CBS and Fox affiliates and a dozen Jacksonville radio stations.

Soon after I get there, a real candidate walks in. I can tell he's a politician by his blue shirt and red tie. He's there for a 2:45 p.m. taping.

Immediately he begins making phone calls, and I get a glimpse of what being a candidate actually entails. He's just come from an event in Savannah, "which went so-so," he tells whomever he's talking to.

I hear him get directions to a 4:30 p.m. newspaper interview in Valdosta and then a homebuilders' dinner in Macon.

When he gets off the phone, he tells me he's the Libertarian candidate for U.S. senator from Georgia, "running to shrink the size of government."

Jessica, the elections producer, comes to take me into the studio. The set is two chairs half-facing each other on a platform. In the background is a big logo for CBS Election '04. I guess the viewers are going to see my jeans and sneakers after all.

Paige Kelton, the local anchor, comes in and complains the studio is too cold. I was sort of hot myself, but they turn off the AC.

Paige is blond and crisp and seems smart. I'm sure this is easy for her.

She tells me to be brief and I ask her if I'll have a blinking red light like on the Bush-Kerry debate.

"No," she says. "I'll just give you a look and you'll know to wrap it up."

My heart is beating fast as they mike me up and I count to ten for the sound check.

I haven't prepared at all. I figured I'd just try to be natural. At the moment that seems like a big mistake.

Paige's first question: Why am I running for Congress?

I tell her I'm running to provide liberal Democrats who'll be voting for John Kerry for president and Betty Castor for senator an alternative to voting for Rep. Crenshaw. I mention my opposition to the war, echoing Kerry's "colossal mistake" remark, and I see Paige is giving me that look.

Next question: What will I do about the budget deficit?

I talk about rescinding Bush's tax cuts for the wealthy.

The next question is what I would do to improve education.

I mention I've been teaching college courses for 30 years and discuss the lack of funding for No Child Left Behind and say there's too much emphasis on standardized tests.

Now we come to a question from a viewer. Paige motions that I should look at some videotape rolling on a nearby monitor.

It's the best possible question for me. A middle-aged black man asks, "How are you going to get our troops out of Iraq?"

I call for immediate withdrawal and say no more Americans should be sacrificing their lives.

Paige follows up by asking if I was always against the war, and I tell her I went to my first anti-war demonstration in February 2002.

It's a gaffe; actually, it was a year later.

Then come the quick get-to-know-me-as-a-person questions. I'm kind of surprised by my own answers.

Growing up, which person influenced me most?

"My grandparents."

Why?

"They came here as children from other countries and became Americans."

Who's my favorite writer?

"Miss Flannery O'Connor of Milledgeville, Georgia," I find myself saying.

That would be a great answer if I were, like the next guy up, trying to replace Zell Miller.

It's finally over, and Paige says it went very well. They run the tape to make sure they've got it, and it looks fine. I shake Paige's hand and Jessica comes to see me out. Jessica says I sounded articulate.

Relieved and elated, I rush over to the UNF campus to catch an appearance by Ralph Nader. He's an hour late, they say, delayed by traffic on his way from South Florida.

Wait a minute. I flew to Jacksonville but Ralph Nader can't afford a plane ticket?

When Nader does come, he sounds petulant and pathetic. There are only about 50 people in the audience.

In the evening I attend a rally in Metropolitan Park, next to Alltel Stadium, where Super Bowl XXXIX will be held next winter.

I fight my shyness and tell someone in charge that I'm running against Rep. Crenshaw. That gets me a seat in the first row, but only if I promise to jump to my feet and yell a lot when Michael Moore appears. They're filming his "Slacker Uprising" tour and the audience has to look enthusiastic.

I don't have to feign enthusiasm in this throng of maybe 2,000.

Rep. Corrine Brown, a spellbinder herself, introduces her "new best friend," and to frenzied applause, Moore comes out in his baseball cap, sweatshirt, and jeans.

For the next hour, Moore tosses out red meat to a pumped-up crowd. He mocks Bush mercilessly. He throws packets of ramen noodles and clean underwear to slackers as incentives to vote.

He rouses all of us, saying this year we're going to win. I look around at the diverse crowd and start to get misty-eyed.

Later, as the rally breaks up amid loud music and cheering, I shake hands with Corrine Brown. She wishes me good luck in my campaign, although I'm not sure she understands that I'm running to be her colleague in Congress.

Then I go back to my motel room and collapse.

How do real candidates do this and a lot more?

- - - -

Sunday, October 3

On the plane coming back from Jacksonville, I can't stop second-guessing my responses on the TV interview.

One of Paige's get-to-know-me-as-a-person questions was, "What do you like most about living in Florida?"

Should I really have said, "The hurricanes"?

- - - -

61

Monday, October 4

It's that time again: I've got to file the financial report of my principal campaign committee, Democrat Grayson for the House, for the quarter ending September 30.

I haven't filled in so many boxes with zeros since I was an 11-year-old watching the '62 Mets at Shea Stadium.

Along with the forms, the Federal Election Commission has sent the September issue of the 12-page *FEC Record*, which contains such exciting features as "Nonfilers," informing readers that The Friends of John Conyers Committee failed to file a 12-day pre-primary report for the August 3 Michigan Democratic primary.

Another feature, "Advisory Opinions," contains a ruling that it's OK for The Friends of Joe Lieberman Committee to buy "a few hundred of the thousands of remainder copies" of the Senator's book for $3.40 per copy and give them away to campaign contributors.

I sympathize with other authors in politics. But at least Senator Lieberman's friends buy his books before giving them away.

I have the opposite problem: I give my friends copies of my books and they sell them to the Strand Book Store.

- - - -

Tuesday, October 5

I mail out 200 copies of this letter to the Baymeadows office of State Farm Insurance:

Dear State Farm Associate,

I know most of you will probably vote Republican and not want to vote for me, but that's OK. I thank you for inviting me to participate in your Candidate Literature Fair.

I am a liberal Democrat who couldn't afford the $9,000 filing fee so I am running as a write-in candidate for Congress in the Fourth District against Rep. Ander Crenshaw, a conservative Republican.

I oppose the war in Iraq and support universal health care and raising the minimum wage. I am in favor of abortion rights, gay rights, and strengthening environmental regulations. (I know I've lost 99% of you already).

I am a State Farm policyholder (car, renter's) and last year when a drunken teen driver totaled my '96 Chevy Cavalier, you gave me more for the car than I'd originally paid for it.

Thanks so much.

Richard Grayson

I still get a lot of offers from companies who want to do target marketing for my campaign, but I can do it myself for free.

- - - -

Wednesday, October 6

Melissa Elsey, the USAVoter Florida team leader, calls to ask why I haven't profiled my campaign on their website. Didn't I get their packet of questions in the mail?

Yes, I tell her, but I've been too busy to respond.

Melissa says thousands of voters will visit the USAVoter website before they enter a voting booth, and that going online to respond will take just a few minutes of my time.

OK, I say. I see that USAVoter is sponsored by the American Policy Roundtable, "a non-profit, non-partisan education and research organization which makes no candidate endorsements, accepts no contributions from campaigns or political parties, nor has it done so since its founding in 1980."

The American Policy Roundtable's headquarters is in Strongville, Ohio.

Doing a little research, I learn that they are really the Ohio Roundtable, a far-right evangelical group whose website features "Protecting Marriage: Church Resources" such as an article titled "Homosexuals and the Next Generation."

Their questions ask candidates their stand on the Federal Marriage Amendment, if *Roe v. Wade* is "good public policy for the United States," and if Congress "should do more to regulate tribal casinos in America."

They ask me to download a "full bio." I don't have time, so I write:

"I prefer to remain an International Man of Mystery."

Their last question asks me to list the three leaders I most admire. I write:

"John Waters, Howard Stern, Jenna Jameson."

On the other end of the political spectrum, I get a copy of the 2004 Voters Guide of the Tallahassee League of Pissed Off Voters, a group dedicated to "kicking stupid white men of all intelligence levels, races and genders out of office."

They urge voters to "help us choose what candidates most represent *us*!" and to "Holla at us and get down with the League!"

In the Fourth Congressional District race, they list candidates' position on 14 issues, such as "abolish death penalty," "renewal of assault weapon ban," and "affirmative action."

Everything that Crenshaw supports, I oppose. Everything that I support, Crenshaw opposes.

- - - -

Thursday, October 7

I have one of those horrible days known to every office worker. Everything goes wrong, from overlooked deadlines to spreadsheets that have vanished into the digital ether. Seven irate people show up at my desk, demanding I do the impossible.

And the more frazzled I get, the more the candidate surveys just keep on a-comin'.

An e-mail questionnaire, "Twenty Top Questions for Central Florida Candidates," contains queries such as "What would you do to improve transportation in Orlando?"

The gerrymandered Fourth District may stretch 170 miles from Jacksonville to Tallahassee, but no part of it is near Orlando, so I hit the delete button.

Americans for Technology Leadership wants to know if I "think the European Commission has gone too far by asking for antitrust sanctions that would prevent Microsoft from improving Windows and adding new features."

I'm getting testy, so I write:

"What does it matter what *I* think anyway? Congress has no control over the European Commission, and if you didn't know that, you're *dumb*."

I have to stay late at the office. When I finally get to my car, it won't start. Rather than deal with the AAA at this hour, I just walk home.

Stopping off at the mailbox, I collect the usual credit-card bills with minimum payments I can barely afford.

But I also spot an envelope from the National Organization for Women Political Action Committee in Washington.

Inside is a letter that begins:

"We are pleased to inform you that because of your strong commitment to feminist issues, the National Organization for Women Political Action Committee, a multi-candidate committee, has endorsed your candidacy for election to the United States House of Representatives. NOW/PAC is proud to endorse those candidates who have been leaders in the struggle to achieve full equality for women."

It goes on to give me the phone extension of NOW's political director if I need to consult with her during my campaign.

It's signed, "For equality, Kim Gandy, Chair," and she's written by hand, in ink:

"Best of luck in November!"

I react like a typical man. I start sobbing.

- - - -

Friday, October 8

I get a questionnaire from a group I can relate to, the Farm Animal Reform Movement (FARM). My responses include the following:

"Yes, I would ban veal crates and sow gestation stalls. I'd ban veal marsala from restaurant menus if I could. Two years ago I worked as part of Floridians for Humane Farms to support a state constitutional amendment banning sow gestation stalls. In my book, these disgusting stalls just aren't kosher, and I'm glad we don't have them in Florida so that in our state, pregnant pigs can turn around to their heart's content."

"Yes, I would ban battery cages for laying hens. Pictures of bald and bleeding battery hens make me want to puke."

"Yes, I support regulation of emissions and antibiotics in factory farms. I understand that the evil corporations that run these places have a right to conduct business under our present system. As to their complaints that these and other regulations will cost more, I say yes, it does cost more to treat animals and humans properly, but that is the price of living in what is supposed to be a civilized society. Vegans rule!!!"

I think being a congressional candidate is really starting to get to me.

I just wish it were the Friday four weeks from now.

By then I'll know the results of this furshlugginer election—and also, on *The O.C.*, whether Ryan is coming back from Chino and where Seth went in that crappy little boat.

- - - -

Saturday, October 9

I get an e-mail from Will, who lives with his wife just outside Tallahassee. They are vegans who hate Rep. Crenshaw because he supports cockfighting.

Will says if the congressman ever comes to town, he's going to stand outside wherever he's appearing with a sign that says "Crenshaw Loves Cock" in big letters and then "Fighting" in tiny print.

Will also says I've got two more votes in Leon County.

This growing support must be what's given me the clout to score a coveted yellow ticket to tonight's town-hall meeting with John Kerry at the Broward Community College gym.

I get there at 5 p.m. and park near the building where I used to teach remedial writing back in the 1980s.

That's when I realize that I have the same amount of clout as 2,500 other Democrats with whom I stand in line for over two hours in the 85-degree heat.

On the other hand, I find I'm entitled to a front-row seat—on the lawn outside the BCC gym once the fire marshals have stopped any more people from entering the building.

Squished between a group of Jamaicans and some octogenarians wearing buttons with "Kerry" written in Hebrew lettering, I watch our presidential candidate on a huge video screen.

Still, TV news cameras are recording us, so I follow orders and wildly wave the big poster I've been given.

It says "Stronger at Home, Respected in the World."

Coming off last night's debate, Kerry looks confident. He repeatedly gets enthusiastic cheers from this crowd, inside and outside the gym.

Kerry puts his arm around his Florida campaign chairman, Rep. Kendrick Meek, and the local candidate for Congress, Debbie Wasserman Schultz. Both of them are in safe Democratic districts.

Kerry says that when he's president, he'll need a Congress he can work with. I worry about a House of Representatives where Republicans like Ander Crenshaw are in the majority. Will they let him govern?

But I've got to push my worries aside. I need to join the rest of the crowd in cheering and clapping and waving my sign for the 11 p.m. news.

- - - -

Monday, October 11

I spend the morning trolling the Web, looking for e-mail addresses of voters in the Fourth Congressional District. I figure the best bets to contact are African-Americans, Democratic activists, college students, and people in the gay community.

I get this quick response from Gwen, head of the College Democrats at the University of North Florida:

"Good luck. But I wish a real candidate would have given Crenshaw a run for his money."

The treasurer of the Jax Triangle Democratic Caucus writes back that although he hasn't had time to review my positions, "I find the concept of a write-in campaign intriguing."

I'd assumed the Triangle Democratic Caucus was a gay group, but maybe they're a bunch of geometry teachers.

Phil Morton, the Democratic candidate for the Nassau County Soil and Water Conservation Board, writes:

"You the man. I already voted for you absentee and sent your name to the 50 people in my address book. More people voted for the write-in in this district two years ago than any other district. Not a win, but it's something to brag about."

I check the Florida Division of Elections results for November 2002 and see that Phil is correct.

Write-in candidates ran in 10 congressional districts. Someone identified only as "B.B.B." got 5 votes running against Democratic Rep. Alcee Hastings. Other write-in candidates, all of whom had both first and last names, got 4, 10, 16, 18, 19, 22, 53, and 73 votes.

But Charles S. Knause, running against Rep. Crenshaw in the Fourth District, managed to garner 509 votes, 0.3 percent of the total votes cast.

That's a lot better than Crenshaw's 2000 write-in opponent, Vince W. Ray, who got zero votes. I guess he didn't live in the district, either.

I can't imagine over 500 people writing me in.

If I get that many votes, I'll have to call for an investigation of yet another case of Florida election fraud.

- - - -

Tuesday, October 12

At the mailbox, I find a letter with the return address "Congress of the United States."

There's no stamp on the envelope, just the signature of Rep. Bob Ney.

Why am I getting mail from a Republican congressman from Ohio?

It turns out he's chairman of the House Administration Committee and he wants to inform me of "some dates you will need to reserve **now** so that you will be available to attend these events if your bid for Congress succeeds."

First of all, I need to "expect to be in Washington from November 13 through November 19 for the New Member Orientation Program." The House will reimburse travel and lodging costs for each member-elect and one designated staff aide.

"Spouses are also invited and encouraged to attend portions of the program," Rep. Ney goes on to say. "However, their travel is not reimbursable by the House. Please note that spouses may not be appointed as the designated aide."

I also need to reserve next January 6-9 to attend "Legislative Issues and Procedures: The CRS Seminar for New Members." CRS is the Congressional Research Service of the Library of Congress.

"This seminar will be held in historic Williamsburg, Virginia, and the program will focus on those issues most likely to be considered in the first six months of the 109th Congress," Rep. Ney writes, assuring me that the program will be "balanced and bipartisan."

Finally, I'm given two phone numbers of House Administration Committee staff, one for "majority," the other for "minority."

The Democrats need a net win of a dozen seats to be in the majority. I guess if that happens, the committee staff members will switch phone numbers.

The Cato Institute is also preparing for the possibility of my election. They send me 30 pages of material explaining why, as a congressman, I should vote to privatize Social Security.

- - - -

Wednesday, October 13

I get an e-mail with the subject line "Hello from the Fourth District."

It's from Ann, who once received a copy of my third book of short stories as a gift. (Since the book retails for $4.99, Ann obviously has at least one very cheap friend.)

Ann says that "it was a bizarre feeling" to discover that I was running for Congress in her district.

"I am not sure whether I wish you were a more 'serious' candidate for our district," Ann writes. "I got totally burned out throwing myself headlong into the Dean campaign here, and haven't fully recovered, so if you were actually out there kissing hands and shaking babies, I might feel compelled to volunteer for you or something."

No American candidate today would kiss hands. It's way too French.

- - - -

Thursday, October 14

At 8 p.m. I call a Jacksonville radio station, WNNR AM 790, to speak with the talk-show host Andy Johnson. A former Democratic state legislator, Andy sued the state in the early 1990s when these malapportioned congressional seats were first created.

Tonight he calls them "a Republican trick to cram all the Democrats into a few districts," like Corrine

Brown's. If northeast Florida had two compact congressional districts, Andy says, both would be Democratic seats.

Andy's a voluble guy, an archenemy of Jacksonville Republicans and a thorn in the side of the Jacksonville mayor. He calls Rep. Crenshaw "a worthless human being who is too busy playing golf to answer calls, letters, or e-mails from anyone who is not one of the fat cats contributing to his campaign."

I try to sound equally blustery and do some bashing of my own, talk-radio style. Not for nothing was I in the Midwood High School Drama Club.

Just before Andy goes to a commercial, he loudly repeats my name at least seven times, spelling it out twice so voters can properly write it in.

This is Florida, after all. If they want their votes to be counted, people better make sure they dot the "i" in "Richard."

- - - -

Friday, October 15

I get 15 e-mails bearing the subject line "Protect Kids From Big Tobacco!"

All of them have the same four paragraphs telling me how I "can be a leader in reducing tobacco's toll."

They remind me of the four identical messages I got in August, which were also about tobacco regulation.

The writers, all of whom are Fourth District voters with addresses in Jacksonville or Lake City, have apparently gotten my name from a website called Kids Before Profits.

I send them back a message discussing my stands on tobacco issues. I remind them that Rep. Crenshaw voted for the mammoth corporate tax giveaway that passed Congress this week.

This bill rewarded tobacco farmers and absentee tobacco landlords with a $10 billion buyout program. House Republicans killed even the minimal regulation on tobacco that the nation's biggest cigarette maker had agreed to.

I address each voter by name and close by saying something about the neighborhood where she lives.

For example, I tell the people in Lake City that I used to visit my friend Terrence there and that Terrence would say that growing up as a black gay kid in Lake City, he didn't get as much grief as you might expect.

I add that the owners of the Travelodge on U.S. 90 by I-75, Mr. and Mrs. Patel, always treated Terrence and me very nicely, and that none of us smoked.

It's important to make personal connections with each voter.

- - - -

Saturday, October 16

A few days ago I got another letter from the Department of Defense's Federal Voting Assistance Program, inviting me to record a message for military families and other U.S. citizens residing overseas.

Since they never used the message I recorded this summer, I was dubious. But I figured that was a typical Pentagon screwup, like Abu Ghraib, so I tried again.

The letter said, "Usually within one business day, your message will be placed in its proper slot and may be heard by citizens calling the DoD Voting Information Center."

But when I call today and make my way through the confusing phone menu, there's still no message from me.

However, voters can hear a message from Rep. Crenshaw telling them that strengthening national defense is his first priority.

"Unfortunately," Crenshaw says, "during the previous administration, our administration took an eight-year defense-procurement holiday."

He explains how he's working hard to make up for that now, spending money right and left (mostly right) as a member of the House Armed Services Committee.

That's how this Pentagon voting hotline got funded.

- - - -

Sunday, October 17

This morning, in bed, wearing only my boxers, I cast my vote.

In the 1980s, when I spent half the year in Manhattan and half the year in Florida, I started voting by absentee ballot. I haven't voted at a polling place since.

I used to have to give some reason why I was requesting an absentee ballot, so I always said I had to be out of town on primary or election day. Now no one has to give a reason to vote by mail.

Voting by mail is an alternative to the electronic voting machines where there is no paper trail. On the mail-in ballot, you fill in ovals with a black pen or pencil.

I can't vote for myself, of course, because I don't live in the Fourth Congressional District, but I look at the instructions for write-in votes:

"To vote for a candidate whose name is not printed on the ballot, fill in the oval, and write in the candidate's name on the blank line provided for a write-in candidate."

"Para votar por un candidato cuyo nombre y apellido no estén impresos en la boleta, llene el impresos en la boleta, llene el óvalo y escriba el nombre y apellido de dicho candidato en el renglón en blanco provisto para candidates que no consten en la boleta."

I have this bad feeling that some people who write in *mi nombre y apellido* will forget to fill in the oval. And then writing my name in probably won't count.

The return envelope for my ballot says I should put 60 cents postage on it. But inside, the instructions say I should put 83 cents postage on the envelope.

Uh-oh. I've got a bad feeling about this.

I put three 37-cent Thurgood Marshall stamps on the envelope, hoping that my investment of $1.11 will ensure that Dr. Brenda C. Snipes, the Broward County Supervisor of Elections, receives my ballot.

What happens after that is anybody's guess.

Starting tomorrow, Floridians can go to polling places to cast their ballots in person.

I prefer voting for Democrats in my underwear.

- - - -

Monday, October 18

Today's the deadline for me to send out my Oct. 1-13 Twelve-Day Pre-General Report of Receipts and Disbursements to the Federal Election Commission, so I again get to practice writing zeros.

The Crenshaw for Congress Committee, like mine, has no debt. But as of the quarter ending September 30, it has $580,841 cash on hand.

Even after winning the GOP primary with 90 percent of the vote, and facing only me in the general election, Crenshaw kept collecting money in September: $1,000 from the Bell South Employees Federal PAC, $4,000 from the National Association of Realtors, $2,500 from the American Medical Association, and $1,000 from the R.J. Reynolds Tobacco Company.

Some of Crenshaw's biggest contributors are political action committees of military contractors: General Electric, Lockheed Martin, Northrop Grumman, and Raytheon.

Other big donors to Crenshaw's campaign are large banks, telecommunications companies, homebuilders, Wal-Mart, UPS, and FedEx.

Meanwhile, early voting begins and people are complaining that Duval County's half-a-million voters should have more than one polling site. The site is deep in the Fourth Congressional District and far away from any African-American neighborhoods.

Coincidentally, John Stafford, the Duval County supervisor of elections, picks this afternoon to resign for health reasons.

But not to worry: Gov. Jeb Bush quickly appoints Bill Scheu as a replacement supervisor of elections. Scheu will take office tomorrow.

Tonight he has to resign as treasurer of the Crenshaw for Congress Committee.

- - - -

Tuesday, October 19

After months of trying to get the attention of someone at Jacksonville's only daily newspaper, the *Times-Union*, I finally get calls from two people there.

Marilyn Young, the metro editor, phones to ask for my e-mail address so she can send me a questionnaire for an online voters' guide. Nin-Hai Tseng, a staff writer, says she needs to interview me for the paper for their election edition on Sunday, October 31.

The interview with Nin is disappointing. She doesn't want to know my positions, just my age, where I got my four college degrees, and if I have a wife and children. Nin seems especially interested in the exact title I have at my day job. She asks me to send her a headshot.

In the evening, I listen online to *The Church of the Left*, a radio show on WOSP hosted by University of North Florida students. They say they're "dirty, poor, bearded, and pierced—just like Jesus."

A disclaimer on their website notes, "This show has nothing to do with religion. The title and slogan are used to confuse the hell out of the right-wingers that we go to school with so we are not lynched and burned at the stake. UNF is a very conservative school!"

While they play music that sounds like a rip-off of an old Dead Kennedys song, I disconnect my dial-up and phone the station. I talk to one of the guys, Nick, and mention my write-in campaign.

It turns out Nick already knows about me from my posts to the Jacksonville Activist Network, a group on Yahoo! He says he'll plug my candidacy on the show.

But I can't go back online to listen, because I've got to keep the phone line free. I'm waiting for a call from Phil LaPadula, an editor at the Fort Lauderdale *Gay Express News*, who wants to interview me.

One of these days I should get either broadband access to the Internet or a cell phone.

While I'm at it, I probably should also get cable TV so I can watch *The Daily Show*, whatever that is.

- - - -

Wednesday, October 20

The Florida State University Students United for Peace and Justice slate is out today. The group is handing out flyers endorsing candidates: John Kerry, Betty Castor, and all Democrats except for one pro-choice Republican state-Senate candidate ("Her Democratic opponent is even more conservative!").

In the Second Congressional District, which takes in most of Tallahassee, they've endorsed moderate Democratic Rep. Alan Boyd: "pro-affirmative action, against Bush's tax cuts for the rich, against private school vouchers."

In the Fourth Congressional District, in eastern Tallahassee, they've endorsed me: "pro-choice, pro-affirmative action, no Iraq war, fair trade, no death penalty, no more drug war, gun control."

In the evening, I get a couple of phone calls. One is from Chiquita, who's putting together a voter guide for what my friends and I back in the day called "right-on people."

Chiquita wants to know if I think felons should get back their right to vote sooner.

I say yes, that Florida's present law is merely a good way for Republicans to disenfranchise poor people who have served their time. It also disenfranchises hundreds of voters who somehow find themselves on the state's notoriously inaccurate list of felons.

After Chiquita thanks me and hangs up, the phone rings again. It's H. David Warder, the write-in candidate in the Fifth Congressional District.

Warder, a former ditch digger and dump-truck driver on disability, is listed in a 1980s British edition of *The Guinness Book of World Records* as holding the flagpole-sitting record.

He sat on a flagpole for 439 days, 11 hours, and 6 minutes to protest high gas prices. However, by the time of the American edition, a Canadian pole-sitter had broken his record.

Warder says he's spent $4.32 on his campaign, and he's crisscrossing his district, which isn't quite as large as mine. "I don't get invited everywhere," he tells me, "but I always bring the house down." In 2006 he hopes to get on the ballot.

He's calling to talk about the Department of Defense Voting Assistance Program hotline. Warder's recorded message wasn't put on the system, either. But he tells me mine is up—only I'm there as a candidate for president:

"They had a menu for Democrats, Republicans, other parties, and then 'not affiliated with a party'—so I thought I'd listen to what Ralph Nader had to say. But it wasn't Nader, it was you talking about running for Congress."

"If I were you," Warder says, "I wouldn't complain. A lot more people will hear you this way. You might even get write-in votes in other districts—but not mine, I hope."

No wonder Rep. Carolyn Maloney—a New York Democrat with whom I once shared a Manhattan cab ride—has called for the Government Accountability Office to examine the Pentagon's mishandling of the Voting Assistance Program.

The GAO better look into it. Or else I guess I'll have to, when I become commander in chief.

- - - -

Thursday, October 21

Back in my office after lunch, I get a call from Susan, who works in a different department.

"Did you make some kind of TV commercial about Iraq?" she asks.

A former co-worker who moved to Bainbridge, Georgia, just phoned Susan to tell her she'd seen me on TV, so I guess Channel 47 has run the interview on the noon news.

I wonder if that zit between my eyebrows distracted viewers.

Later I get a call from Donna at the Florida Division of Elections. She wants to let me know that Duval County has established four additional early-voting sites.

If I want, I can attend accuracy and logistical testing at one of the polling places tomorrow morning.

Too bad I can't make it. I'd like to meet the new supervisor of elections to find out how he'll make sure any write-in votes for me are counted. And to ask him if he got his money's worth when he contributed $5,000 to Crenshaw's campaign.

- - - -

Friday, October 22

The *Times-Union* online questionnaire is a form that asks 11 questions and lets me reply at length— provided each answer is "no more than 220 characters."

So I have to stifle my inner blowhard:

Q: What should America's strategy be regarding the war in Iraq?
A: The war in Iraq was a catastrophic mistake. We should remove all U.S. troops as expeditiously as possible. No more Americans should die in this idiotic conflict.

Q: The mother of a soldier killed in Iraq asks you, "Why did my child have to die in the war?" What is your response?
A: Your child died because people believed in the lies of a president and his administration. Your child was a

85

heroic individual sacrificed by evil people in the name of empire.

Q: What will constitute a victory in the war on terrorism and how can it be accomplished?
A: There is no "war" on terrorism any more than there is, or should be, a "war" on drugs. Al Qaeda attacked us on 9/11. Terrorism was merely the means they chose to accomplish that attack.

Q: How can prescription-drug costs for consumers be reduced?
A: We should do what most other countries do: impose price controls. The drug companies are making obscene profits off sick people.

Q: How will you protect Florida's military bases in the upcoming BRAC process?
A: They shouldn't be protected if the nonpartisan panel believes they are wasteful and need to be closed. Let's get the military contractors off welfare.

And so on.

An hour after I submit the form, I get an e-mail congratulating me because my answers have been approved for publication by *Times-Union* editors.

What a disappointment.

- - - -

Saturday, October 23

The *Express Gay News* story comes out. After glancing at my photo on the front page, I kick myself for not sending them a pic of Chad Michael Murray instead.

Then I move on to deconstructing the article. It begins:

"Jim Stork's demise as a congressional candidate was a disappointment to many gay voters. But some Floridians will still have a chance to vote for a gay candidate for Congress."

We've come a long way from 1950, when George Smathers could turn North Florida voters against Sen. Claude Pepper by calling Pepper a shameless extrovert whose sister was a thespian and whose brother was a *Homo sapiens*.

I don't even think Smathers's charges that Pepper matriculated with co-eds, practiced celibacy before marriage and monogamy afterwards, and vacillated one night on the Senate floor, would affect today's voters in the slightest.

The article quotes me on my political philosophy:

"'I'm like Charles Foster Kane,' said Grayson. 'I'm a fighting liberal.'"

But it doesn't quote what I said next:

"Only they'll never catch me in a love nest with a 'singer.'"

It dredges up a decade-old Crenshaw interview with the *St. Petersburg Times* in which he says that he didn't know anyone who was gay or lesbian and then notes:

"Repeated phone calls to Crenshaw's campaign manager, Pat Rogers, were never returned."

Crenshaw needs a campaign manager? Running against *me*?

Near the end, the article makes this astonishing assertion:

"Based on his resume, many politicos would probably admit that Grayson is qualified to serve in the Congress."

They would probably admit no such thing. I can't even imagine anyone admitting to being a "politico."

- - - -

Sunday, October 24

The *Times-Union* runs Nin-Hai Tseng's story on local congressional races with a headline about the one contested Democrat-Republican race in the area: in the Sixth Congressional District, where Rep. Cliff Stearns, a Republican, is again facing his 2002 opponent, Democrat David Bruderly.

The article notes that Corrine Brown and Ander Crenshaw have only write-in opponents. Rep. John Mica, a Republican in the Seventh District, has no opposition and is not on the ballot.

There's a little box with my photo and vital stats. It has my party as Democrat and my "office sought" as "write-in candidate, U.S. House, District 4."

Meanwhile, I get another dozen "Protect Kids from Big Tobacco!" e-mails and answer them with my stock reply. Now I add a sentence about Crenshaw's recent contribution from R.J. Reynolds.

It probably won't get the vote of one guy whose Hotmail address includes the phrase "WarriorForChrist," but you never know.

- - - -

Monday, October 25

The postal service brings a manila envelope from the House Administration Committee. I have to go to a password-protected website and upload a "high-resolution official headshot photograph in JPEG format." Should I be elected, this photo will be used to train Capitol police to recognize me.

I also have to give them my marital status, religious affiliation, ADA requirements, and the names of my children and my "spouse/partner." That "partner" surprises me.

I also have to fill out reservation forms for my hotel reservations for the November 13-20 orientation for new members of Congress. A double occupancy rate is $190 a night, and I don't think I have enough available credit on any of my 28 Visas or MasterCards to cover this amount.

Luckily, "the day after the election, the reservation forms for elected winners will be transmitted to the hotel, and the reservation forms for those not attending the orientation will be shredded."

I notice they do not say "losers."

- - - -

Tuesday, October 26

I get a call from Jeff Adelson, a reporter at the *Gainesville Sun*, who wants to interview me for a "very small" story on the Fourth District race. Only a sliver of the district is at the northern edge of the paper's circulation area.

Jeff asks me about my "platform."

"I'm gonna soak the fat boys," I tell him, "and I'm gonna spread it out real thin."

"Excuse me?" Jeff says.

I explain that I'm for taxing the hell out of rich people—not that I have anything against them. After all, without rich people, America would be a poorer place.

When I tell Jeff that I support "socialized medicine," he tells me that he's got a story in today's paper in which Rep. Cliff Stearns accuses his Democratic opponent of favoring "socialized medicine."

"I've never heard anyone use that term except in a negative light," Jeff says.

"Really?" I say. Then I tell him I'm for abortion on demand.

- - - -

Wednesday, October 27

The *Gainesville Sun* headline reads "Campaign Still On for Rep. Ander Crenshaw":

It notes that though Crenshaw handily defeated his opponent in the Republican primary and faces no formal Democratic opposition in the general election, the congressman will be on the Nov. 2 ballot because I filed as a write-in candidate for the district—"which includes parts of Columbia, Duval, Nassau, Baker, Union, Hamilton, Madison, Jefferson and Leon counties."

The story uses the "P" word:

"Grayson said his platform includes calls for withdrawal of troops from Iraq, a $10 minimum wage, a repeal of Bush's tax cuts for the wealthy, socialized medicine and gay marriage."

And it gives me one direct quote:

"'If they're voting for John Kerry for president, they probably don't want to vote for a conservative Republican congressman and should write me in,' Grayson said."

As well as one by the incumbent:

"'The best way to win the war on terror is to continue funding military assets, programs and personnel,' Crenshaw has said at campaign appearances."

The article also quotes a "spokesman" for Crenshaw about his future plans, including a national sales tax to replace the income tax and other Republican ideas.

If my campaign were a one-man Broadway show, it would be called *I Am My Own Spokesman*.

Anyway, it's all to no avail. The voters of the Fourth Congressional District will choose *cojones* over *rachmones* every time.

- - - -

Thursday, October 28

The TriangleJax Democratic Caucus, a group of GLBT Democrats in Duval County, includes me on their list of voting recommendations for members. The same goes for the Jacksonville Area National Organization for Women, which advises voters that they have to write in my name because I'm not on the ballot like John Kerry, John Edwards, Betty Castor, and Corrine Brown.

The problem for me is these slates are just going out and a lot of liberal activists have voted already.

An e-mail arrives from Rob in Jacksonville, saying he would have voted for me but didn't learn about my candidacy until after he'd cast his ballot.

He simply wrote in "Democrat" on the write-in line. That vote won't count.

But then neither will the votes of a lot of other Floridians.

- - - -

Friday, October 29

The *Times-Union* voters' guide will appear in Sunday's paper, but it's already online. Voters can see the contrasts between Ander Crenshaw and what's-his-name:

Occupation: "investment banker" vs. "author and college instructor."

Military experience: "n/a" vs. "draft dodger, 1969-73."

Religion: "Episcopalian" vs. "atheist."

Marital status: "married" vs. "single gay man."

Family: "wife and two daughters" vs. "pet goldfish Frisky."

Experience: "Florida House of Representative, Florida Senate, first Republican elected President of Florida Senate, Member of Congress" vs. "some."

While I call the war in Iraq a catastrophic mistake, Crenshaw says:

"We need to do what we're doing: protect and train Iraqis to defend themselves, rout out terrorists who want to rule by tyranny and continue to bring democracy to a land formerly ruled by a murderous tyrant."

We have different ideas about the affordability of health care:

Crenshaw: "The biggest hurdle is frivolous medical liability lawsuits. The Republican-led House and President Bush tried to enact reform but special interests have stymied efforts in the Senate."

Loser: "We need universal, single-payer coverage. Every other civilized country in the world guarantees its citizens medical care paid for by the government."

And my answer to "How can prescription drug costs for consumers be reduced?" is price controls. This is Crenshaw's answer:

"Over 4.1 million low-income senior citizens are already taking advantage of the Medicare Modernization Act enacted last year. Drug re-importation sounds good but currently there is no way to protect Americans from tainted drugs or fraud."

Currently there is no way to protect Americans from political fraud, either.

- - - -

Saturday, October 30

Today I'm doing something more important than my own silly little race. At the Lauderhill Mall in my old neighborhood, I'm a "poll presence," helping the thousand or so Broward County voters—nearly all of them African-

and Caribbean-American—waiting on line for early voting.

The line is so long that it snakes outside the mall. I fetch bottles of water for people and get folding chairs for the frail retirees, including an elderly Jamaican man who tells me he was a New York bus driver.

"Like Ralph Kramden," I say, but either he doesn't hear or didn't watch *The Honeymooners*. "Which bus?"

"Mostly Utica Avenue in Brooklyn," he says.

"The B-46," I say, and he nods.

There don't seem to be any Republicans challenging their eligibility. Only three black Republicans are in evidence, holding their Bush/Cheney posters in silence.

Taunting them are a group of 10-year-old boys who chant, "Bush is scary, Vote for Kerry!" Somehow they make it rhyme.

Several people are wearing T-shirts that say "ALCEE'S TEAM FOR KERRY."

In 1991, when I came out of a courtroom after my bankruptcy hearing, the first person I saw was former federal judge Alcee Hastings, who'd been forced off the bench because of an alleged bribe.

In the elevator, I told him about my bankruptcy.

"You'll bounce back," Hastings told me. "People always do."

The next year, Hastings himself bounced back by getting elected to the House, becoming a member of the body that had voted 413-3 to impeach him.

When my plantar fasciitis starts to bother me from standing so long, I head over to the Starbucks run by the Magic Johnson Development Corporation. The barista knows me and my usual: a venti unsweetened black iced tea.

Back home, I check e-mail before watching *Sabado Gigante*.

House Minority Leader Nancy Pelosi has sent me a message with the subject line "Last Chance for Victory." She asks me to "make a contribution now to help elect John Kerry and our Democratic House candidates."

God help me, I think I'm one of them.

- - - -

Sunday, October 31

I intend to go to canvassing for Kerry at 1 p.m., I really do, but I slept only four hours last night. So I lie down for just a minute, which turns out to be a two-hour nap.

What if Kerry loses Florida, and the presidency, by the number of votes I would have gotten to the polls had I not been so lazy? For the next four years I'll feel guilty—I mean, a *lot* more guilty than I usually do.

Don't genuine candidates ever want to take a day off to rest? I guess not if it's a close contest. But, hey, it's Halloween and the Crenshaw/Grayson race isn't exactly a smackdown on the order of Freddy vs. Jason.

American campaigns are months too long. In England, I could stand for Parliament as a candidate of the Monster Raving Loony Party and it would all be over in six weeks.

Tired of politics, I go downtown to this club Revolution to see Taking Back Sunday, Fall Out Boy, and Matchbox Romance.

It's an "all ages" show, but most of the crowd is too young to vote. I'd have more confidence in our democracy if they could.

Everyone seems to pretend I'm not over 50 except for one girl, Amber, who mistakes me for her friend Brittany's dad.

Back home at midnight, my exhilaration from the night's music dissipates when I see that a *Times-Union* reader has mistaken me for a serious candidate. He writes:

"You don't know me, but I am one of the people who work for the government as an aircraft mechanic at one of those military installations. And I think that you don't know what you are talking about. You have no experience in how to work in politics, you may feel that the war is wrong, and that is your right as an American citizen whose rights have been protected by previous generations of people like me from the beginning of this country until today. It is my considered opinion that you could not even hold the job of dogcatcher."

He signs it, "Respectfully."

I write back, thanking him for his note, urging that he vote for Rep. Crenshaw, and agreeing that I would indeed make a terrible dogcatcher.

I can't even catch the baby lizards that keep sneaking into my apartment when I open the front door.

- - - -

Monday, November 1

The lines at early voting are not as long as on the weekend, but they're still pretty long. I hand out CDs titled *Wake Up Everybody*, produced by Babyface and Russell Simmons and featuring everyone from Wyclef Jean and Mary J. Blige to Reverend Run and Missy Elliott.

I've also got the Florida Voter's Bill of Rights to hand out, but I haven't seen anyone trying to stop people from voting. The two out-of-state lawyers originally assigned to monitor here have been sent to canvass voters for tomorrow.

I wonder how things are going in the Fourth Congressional District, but it's too late for me to do much for my own candidacy except e-mail a whole lot of people.

The only message I get today is from another voter who read about me in the *Times-Union*. But he lives in Georgia and he wants to ask me for advice on how he can run for Congress in 2006.

I hope that two years from now, there will be credible Democrats on the ballot in every Florida congressional-district race.

Ideally, they would be people with experience in the state legislature or local office—or else millionaires with lots of money to blow on a campaign.

Imagine what I could have done with loads of cash to spend on TV commercials.

That kind of media barrage would probably land me in the single digits in tomorrow's vote. As it is, I doubt I'll get 0.1 percent of the vote.

I phone Crenshaw's office to find out where he'll be spending election night so I can call him there and concede.

The receptionist keeps telling me that I can't be running against him, that Congressman Crenshaw is unopposed.

The CNN website agrees with her. Sixty-three members of the U.S. House of Representatives—15 percent of the total—face no major party opponent tomorrow.

- - - -

Tuesday, November 2

On Election Day 40 years ago, I stood on the corner of Avenue N and East 56th Street in Brooklyn, just across the street from the American Legion post that served as our neighborhood polling place.

99

I handed out leaflets with the same slogan pasted on every telephone pole around: "Get on the Johnson, Humphrey, Kennedy Team."

Backing me up were three 11-year-old girls chanting, "Goldwater in '64, hot water in '65, bread and water in '66." Would-be hecklers, this trio from Mary Queen of Heaven School didn't realize their refrain was not complimentary to the Republican candidate, about to lose in a landslide in which two-thirds of congressional seats go to the Democrats.

Forty years later, I'm standing the requisite 50 feet from a Jacksonville polling place, singing a song I learned back in 1964 from Soupy Sales' lion hand puppet Pookie:

Get out and vote!

Get out and vote!

It will raise a lump of glory

In your throat!

I'm handing out homemade leaflets that say, "Get on the Kerry, Edwards, Castor, Grayson Team."

A man refuses to take one but wishes me luck with a capital "F."

I smile at him and reply with another phrase learned in my Brooklyn adolescence: "*Maman-ou genyen yon infestation kriket lan krek li.*"

Other voters want to shake my hand for trying to rid the Fourth Congressional District of its infestation of

Republican officeholders. All of them promise to vote for me. A TV reporter asks me to wave for the cameras. The crowd behind me cheers ...

OK, OK, that's what I *wish* I were doing.

Instead, I'm standing on a median strip in downtown Fort Lauderdale, holding up a sign that says "VOTE FIRE SAFETY BOND."

They already had two people to hold up Kerry/Edwards signs, so I got stuck with this one.

I don't even know who Fire Safety Bond is or what he's running for.

But that's politics: it's a rough life, but capable of honor.

Back home, I find a "Good Luck, Grayson!" e-mail from Rob in Jacksonville.

"You have become quite beloved amongst my circle of friends, which still won't translate into votes for you," he writes. "Maybe someday people who speak as straightforwardly as you can be elected to office ... where? This city? The city where 40,000 turned out for a Bush rally?"

Rob closes, "Thanks for your hard-fought campaign—or at least for running anyway. Also, thanks for turning me on to Taking Back Sunday."

He signs the note, "Your constituent."

On Election Night, I always have the same ritual: I make lots of tea and sit myself down in front of the TV—I have a 13-inch one, with a VCR slot built in, so I have to sit close—and watch the Big Three networks we non-cable people are stuck with.

The best stuff is always on early. Like one year on ABC, after the polls closed in Indiana at 6 p.m., Peter Jennings announced they were projecting a win by Sen. Peter Luger when he meant Sen. Richard Lugar.

That confirmed my belief that eating lots of meat makes people stupid.

Unfortunately, carnivores make up the vast majority of the American electorate. It's going to be a long night.

- - - -

Wednesday, November 3

The people have spoken, the subhuman douche bags.

After 1964, I didn't celebrate another presidential election for a dozen years. I went from being a bar mitzvah boy to a 25-year-old struggling writer and adjunct composition teacher with an M.A. and an M.F.A. I earned $3,300 that year and still lived in Brooklyn with my family.

On a chilly, overcast afternoon the Sunday before Jimmy Carter was elected president that year, I stood in a Carroll Gardens playground, cheering our candidate for senator, Daniel Patrick Moynihan.

Moynihan said there wasn't any point in being Irish if you don't know that the world is going to break your heart eventually.

He got elected back then, in 1976. The next happy presidential election for me was 16 years later, when Clinton got elected the first time. By then I was over 40, a second-year law student in Gainesville, still teaching writing part-time at the local community college.

I saw Bill and Hillary and Al and Tipper on campus when their bus tour came to town. Our evidence professor told us all we could skip class because the election was more important.

All I can recall from that day is how the Clintons and Gores seemed to glow, how beautiful the elderly actress Ruth Warrick—Phoebe on *All My Children*, the first Mrs. Charles Foster Kane from *Citizen Kane*—looked, and how lame River Phoenix's band was. River Phoenix lived in town and was much cuter onscreen than in person, by the way.

The day after the election, I noticed the forlorn faces of the young white guys from the law school's Republican club. They were in their early 20s and the only presidents they knew were Reagan and the just-defeated George H.W. Bush.

I went over to one of them, Michael, whose caustic sense of humor I admired. I told him to buck up. He was an Irish-American, so I quoted Moynihan's line about heartbreak.

The next week, I noticed that the law-school Republican club had called a meeting "to discuss Hillary's latest hairdo disaster."

Two years after that—just 10 years ago, in 1994—I worked my heart out trying to prevent the passage of two referenda in Gainesville. Proposition 1 rescinded the county's gay-rights law. Amendment 1 put into the county charter a provision that forbade us from ever passing another gay-rights law in Alachua County.

Both passed, of course. I knew they would, by a 2-1 margin. But I loved working on that campaign, "No on 1."

We scheduled a "victory" party downtown for Election Night. It was a very gloomy scene. The Republicans swept Congress that year. In Florida, the GOP took over the state legislature. The gay and lesbian kids who were UF undergraduates had their hearts broken.

"It's going to be all right," I told one young guy whom I had this impossible crush on. I told him I thought Amendment 1 was unconstitutional, that it would be struck down. (And that's exactly what happened, following the 1996 Supreme Court decision in *Romer v. Evans*.)

Besides, the numbers were telling us that within the city of Gainesville, our side wasn't doing so badly. We were getting killed in the rural areas of the county, losing 9-1 among the rednecks.

I got on the board of the Human Rights Council of North Central Florida and a political action committee,

Human Rights Action. Within a couple of years, we elected three sympathetic city commissioners, and the city passed its own gay-rights bill.

It's still on the books in Gainesville. As is a domestic partnership registry. And Craig Lowe, who was the president of our gay-rights group, now serves on the city commission.

Craig was unopposed for re-election this year. I wrote him to ask for his endorsement, but I guess he was too busy to get back to me.

Yesterday, another "unopposed" candidate, U.S. Rep. Ander Crenshaw, Republican of the Fourth Congressional District, got 255,448 votes, according to the Florida Division of Elections unofficial Election Night returns.

The same unofficial returns show that a write-in candidate, Richard Grayson, received 1,167 votes.

About the Author

RICHARD GRAYSON is the author of the
short story collections *With Hitler in New York,*
Lincoln's Doctor's Dog, Highly Irregular Stories,
I Brake for Delmore Schwartz, I Survived Caracas
Traffic, The Silicon Valley Diet and *And to Think*
That He Kissed Him on Lorimer Street.

www.ingramcontent.com/pod-product-compliance
Lightning Source LLC
Chambersburg PA
CBHW031322040426
42443CB00005B/182